WAGGONER CARR
NOT GUILTY

WAGGONER CARR
NOT GUILTY

BY

WAGGONER CARR

WITH

JACK KEEVER

COVER BY DON COLLINS

SHOAL CREEK PUBLISHERS, INC.
P. O. BOX 9737   AUSTIN, TEXAS 78766

COPYRIGHT © 1977 BY WAGGONER CARR

All rights in this book are reserved. No part of this book may be used or reproduced in any manner whatsoever without written permission, except in the case of brief quotations embodied in a review.

FIRST EDITION

LITHOGRAPHED AND BOUND IN THE UNITED STATES OF AMERICA

Library of Congress Cataloging in Publication Data
  Carr, Waggoner.
    Waggoner Carr, not guilty.

    1. Carr, Waggoner. I. Keever, Jack, joint author. II. Title.
KF224.C37S5   345'.73'0263   77-23549
ISBN 0-088319-029-X

DEDICATION

I gratefully dedicate this book to my wonderful family, relatives, and friends who so loyally "kept the faith" throughout my dark days of despair, and, who, after victory, helped me back on my feet.

CONTENTS

CHAPTER		PAGE
1	The Hottest News Around	1
2	Lonesome Man	7
3	"And Now as to Waggoner Carr"	13
4	Good Bill	19
5	Some Kind of Deal	25
6	Rushing to Judgment	33
7	My Appeal Fails	39
8	"The No. 1 Case in the Nation"	41
9	"A Fool for a Client"	49
10	There Always Was Tomorrow	53
11	A Close Family	61
12	Crack In The Door	65
13	Will Wilson and a Few Files	75
14	"The Traveling Watergate Show"	83
15	An Honest Man	97
16	A Living Example	111

ILLUSTRATIONS

	Page
Waggoner Carr waves to crowds as he rides in a Houston motorcade in his unsuccessful 1968 race for governor.	3
In 1972, Republican Senator John Tower, a victor over Waggoner Carr in 1966, was worried that Democrat Ben Barnes might take away his job.	6
Guards wait to inspect Waggoner Carr's briefcase in the federal courthouse at Dallas before his first hearing in the suit filed by the U. S. Securities and Exchange Commission.	14
Waggoner Carr smiles at a Houston Gridiron dinner in 1967, with Ben Barnes on his left. Two years later, when Barnes was lieutenant governor, they visited about two banking bills that became part of the Sharpstown Scandal.	22
Houston businessman Frank Sharp is shown in 1971 after he had testified before a federal grand jury in Houston. Sharp testified after pleading guilty to two minor violations and was granted immunity from further state or federal prosecution.	28
Waggoner Carr speaks to reporters in Dallas after federal judge Sarah Hughes placed him under permanent injunction in an alleged stock manipulation scheme.	32
Frank Sharp was the subject of a $100 million damage suit filed by Waggoner Carr. The suit is still pending.	38
Waggoner Carr, former attorney general, is photographed in Dallas after being indicted twice in 1972 for fraud and conspiracy.	43
Waggoner Carr (right) is shown in Dallas with Travis Shelton, a Lubbock lawyer who helped in Carr's defense.	50
Waggoner Carr hesitates before responding to a reporter's question at his 1973 trial in Dallas for fraud and conspiracy.	57

Waggoner Carr again talks to the press in Dallas, after he was acquitted on a 12-count indictment alleging fraud and conspiracy. Behind Carr (left to right) are his wife, Ernestine; his daughter-in-law, Diana; and his son, David.   62

John Osorio (front) and his lawyer, Emmett Colvin, wait for the elevator in the Dallas federal courthouse. Osorio testified at a 1973 hearing that a government prosecutor told him he could escape more indictments if he would say he had bribed Ben Barnes to pass two bank deposit bills.   66

Senator John Tower (left) and Attorney General John Mitchell stand at a Dallas banquet. Both were subpoenaed to appear at a 1973 hearing in connection with Carr's accusations that he was the victim of a Republican plot but only Mitchell came. Tower was excused by a Senate resolution.   78

Former Attorneys General Richard Kleindienst (top) and John Mitchell (bottom) enter the Dallas federal courthouse for the "Traveling Watergate Show" in October 1973.   82

Former U. S. attorney Anthony J. P. Farris of Houston, who filed application in 1971 to grant Frank Sharp immunity from prosecution.   91

Former Governor John Connally (left) wishes Waggoner Carr well after Carr had addressed thousands of supporters in a 1966 Austin campaign speech for the U. S. Senate.   96

Waggoner Carr arrives for his second trial in Dallas — in 1974 — with one of his lawyers, Travis Shelton (left). He was acquitted of all charges.   100

One of the many people who congratulated Waggoner Carr after his second acquittal was Leon Jaworski (left), special prosecutor of the Watergate investigation. This picture was taken in 1966, when Carr was attorney general. On the right is then-U. S. Representative Bob Casey of Houston.   110

PUBLISHER'S FOREWORD

During the holiday season of 1970, Waggoner Carr was thinking of more than Christmas gifts for his family and friends. He had a Texas-sized itch to get back into politics.

His last race, for governor in 1968, had been a losing one, but the political embers were still glowing. His law firm was making money, his campaign debts had been paid and, most gratifying to him, he was being called upon to speak at public gatherings and club meetings over the state. People thought what he had to say was worthwhile. His speeches on respect for the law and the perils of civil disobedience were widely acclaimed.

He also was active as a regent of Texas Tech University, his alma mater, and in the Texas Youth Conference. The conference had grown out of the Attorney General's Youth Conference on Crime, which Carr had started in 1963. He credited those annual conferences for the decline in juvenile crime in 1966—the first time this had happened in the state's history.

That was the year, too, that Carr had been selected by the attorneys general of the other 49 states as the nation's outstanding attorney general of the year.

By 1971, at the age of 54, he had a reputation for honesty, integrity and leadership. For 17 years, he had served in offices of public trust—Lubbock county attorney, state representative, Speaker of the House of Representatives and Texas attorney general. He was the third man in Texas history to be elected Speaker for two consecutive terms.

Suddenly, with the filing of a heavily publicized federal lawsuit that proclaimed he had committed serious criminal acts through schemes and conspiracies, his world collapsed.

It would become a three-year nightmare.

It was during that nightmare that Carr thought, "There's history here," and he jotted down his impressions and collected the factual data that has been put into this book.

Shoal Creek Publishers thinks it is a significant part of Texas history, and we believe you will think so, too.

W. L. THOMPSON

The power to enforce carries with it responsibilities for both zeal and restraint. As enforcement officers must be zealous in seeking out and bringing to justice willful wrongdoers, so they must always police themselves to permit no breach of the fragile line between a free state and a police state.

—Waggoner Carr, excerpt from speech on occasion of his induction into office of Texas Attorney General, January 3, 1963.

1

The Hottest News Around

It was dark, about 6 p.m., and I was saying good-by to several friends and political supporters when the phone rang in my law office at the International Life Building in Austin.

The caller identified himself as an attorney for the U. S. Securities and Exchange Commission in Fort Worth. He curtly informed me that I had been named in a complaint which alleged that I had been part of a complex conspiracy to cheat the public by manipulating the stock of several corporations, notably the National Bankers Life Insurance Co. of Dallas.

I was astonished and asked for details, but he replied that that was all the information he had and that questions would have to be answered by another SEC attorney, Robert Watson, the next morning.

Three or four visitors still lingering in the hall looked in as the caller advised me that the complaint had been filed in federal Judge Sarah T. Hughes's court at Dallas, 200 miles away, and she had set a hearing for 1:30 p.m. the next day.

The calendar on my desk read Monday, January 18, 1971.

It was the eve of the inauguration of Governor Preston Smith and Lt. Governor Ben Barnes to their second terms in office. Thousands of Democrats were in Austin for the "Victory Dinner" Monday night, and my wife, Ernestine, and I had planned to go.

I had invited a dozen or so campaign leaders from my previous races to discuss whether I should run for statewide office in 1972. It had been a jolly reunion, and I was feeling good.

I had lost my last two races, as the Democratic nominee against Republican John Tower for the U.S. Senate in 1966 and for governor in 1968, but I had finished third among ten candidates for governor after running a poor-boy campaign with only $100,000 to spend. The other six major candidates all spent more, with two spending nearly $700,000 each. My new law firm of Carr, Osorio, Palmer, Long and Coleman was showing good promise and I had paid all my campaign debts.

For months, I had been speaking to youth groups, trying to get them to settle down in face of all the rioting against the Vietnam War, and I almost had more speech invitations than I could handle. The statewide publicity had been miraculous, both in front-page stories and editorials, and I had been asked by a substantial number of people to get back into politics.[1]

My old teammates that evening were especially enthusiastic about the idea. They had begun to smell the smoke and wanted to head for the fire. I had plenty of time, however, so we decided to feel out voter sentiment before I made a final decision. I think the odds were that I would have made it into the 1972 lieutenant governor's race.[2]

Suddenly the phone call. It was the end of the world. The timing was explosive. Everything was rosy, then an abrupt abyss, a darkness that was unbelievable.

What in the devil was going on? I couldn't tell my visitors about the call. It would have blown the meeting sky-high, and they would have dispersed the talk as the hottest news around.

If the news I had gotten about the complaint was true, just the news—whether or not it was factual—it would blow me out of any political race. To talk about it was a waste of time.

Within minutes, even before I had a chance to call my wife and tell her we were cancelling out on the "Victory Dinner," I started getting local and long-distance calls from reporters firing questions and demanding explanations. My answer to the first caller was, "I don't know what they're talking about; let me try to find out what's going on and I'll call you back."

I tried to jot down the name of each caller—the Associated Press in Dallas, a Wichita Falls television station, The Houston

PHOTO: HOUSTON *CHRONICLE*

WAGGONER CARR WAVES TO CROWDS AS HE RIDES IN A HOUSTON MOTORCADE IN HIS UNSUCCESSFUL 1968 RACE FOR GOVERNOR.

Post, the Houston *Chronicle,* Texas State Network, a Fort Worth radio-television station and others.

As the reporters called, I asked them what they knew about the suit, and I was finally able to write a statement, which I read to each caller:

"Recently I have been associated with various businesses in which a lot of well-known businessmen of Texas were involved. There were many transactions carried out over which I had no knowledge or control. I was personally not involved in any stock trading in the companies mentioned in the complaint. I am sure the hearing will bear this out."

This, a lawyer would say, was a general denial.

The "Victory Dinner" had started, but I had no intention of going because I knew I would be subjected to questions by hundreds of people who had heard the news on radio or television. I needed to be busy about my business.

I didn't get home until 9:30 that night. I told my wife what had happened and that I had to be in Dallas the next day. Someone had suggested that I should try to get Barefoot Sanders to represent me in court. Barefoot and I had been friends since the legislature, when I was a member and later Speaker and he was a House member from Dallas. Afterward, we'd run into each other at social activities and in political campaigns.[3] We were not close, but we were not strangers either. I called his home, and his wife told me he was out of pocket.

I didn't sleep well that night and I was on the road to Dallas by daybreak, with a three-hour drive to think about what had happened. Two things seemed obvious: the Nixon administration had timed the suit to get the greatest shock effect on Texas Democrats, and it had taken great pains to see that the news was fed to the public as swiftly as possible. The case was the lead story in the evening news broadcasts and hit the top headlines in the morning papers. I felt as if I were being crushed by black headlines proclaiming that I had committed serious criminal acts.

The character assassins had come to Texas.

It was later revealed in sworn testimony that the SEC office in Fort Worth had received a telephone call from Washington instructing lawyers to file the case on the politically sensitive date of January 18. The complaint was so hurriedly drafted that it had numerous typing errors which had been corrected by pen. The figure $3 million, for example, came out $300 million in the typed copy.

I stopped at a gas station on the outskirts of Dallas and called Barefoot's office, and luckily he was there. I remember him saying later as I sat down, "You have a problem, don't you Waggoner?"

"Yeah," I replied, "I have a problem and I want you to help me if you can."

He agreed to represent me at the hearing and to pick up a copy of the pleadings, which were an inch thick. I didn't go to Judge Hughes's court; none of the defendants was there in person. As expected, the judge granted the SEC request for a temporary restraining order. This merely meant that everything connected with the companies and persons named in the suit had to be held in *status quo* until a hearing could be held to determine if there was any substance to the government's accusations.

She set a hearing for February 8. That gave me three weeks to get ready.

When Barefoot returned from the courthouse, I saw for the first time a copy of the complaint. It charged that 15 persons, including myself, and 13 companies had schemed to sell unregistered stocks, drain companies of their assets, issue bad checks, misrepresent financial conditions, bribe legislators and generally conduct a giant shell game that boggled the mind.

Barefoot told me that he and his law partners had decided, for reasons which they did not reveal to me, that he could go no further in the case.[4] He said he wouldn't charge me for his services at the courthouse.

Reflecting on that first hectic day, I think of what Bill Morse, a Houston lawyer who had attended the political meeting the night before in my office, later said to me.

"Waggoner," he said, "that was the shortest campaign in history."

PHOTO: HOUSTON *CHRONICLE*

IN 1972, REPUBLICAN SENATOR JOHN TOWER, A VICTOR OVER WAGGONER CARR IN 1966, WAS WORRIED THAT DEMOCRAT BEN BARNES MIGHT TAKE AWAY HIS JOB.

2

Lonesome Man

Like most who have been in politics, I have experienced victories and defeats, but the searing disappointment of defeat and the remorse over wasted time, money and effort cannot compare with the hell that descended on me when the SEC loosed its broadside. It is a shattering experience to have a good name and a good reputation blown to bits by a powerful federal government agency that has embarked on a political vendetta.

It was only later, however, that I would learn for certain of this vendetta. Here is some background.

When John Connally, the former Democratic governor of Texas, became a member of President Nixon's cabinet in 1970, Senator John Tower apparently became worried that Connally would upstage him; Texans who wanted to contact Nixon would go through Connally, not Tower. Even more threatening to Tower was the possibility that Barnes would run against him in 1972. Barnes was Connally's protégé, and Connally's presence in the cabinet should make it easier for Barnes to garner money and votes. Barnes could argue convincingly that as senator he would have an inroad with the Republican President, as well as the Democratic Congress. This would be unbearable for Tower.

By that time, U. S. Attorney General John Mitchell had, for all practical purposes, taken charge of the Committee to Re-elect the President, and Tower and his state campaign finance chairman, Julian Zimmerman of Austin, Texas, went to see Mitchell in December 1970. The Connally-Barnes relationship, they told Mitchell, could damage Tower's chances, as well as cut into Nixon's vote in Texas.

Mitchell told Tower and Zimmerman that an investigation was being conducted in Texas that "could conceivably" affect the political picture in the state and Tower should not worry about Barnes as he would be eliminated as a Texas political force by the investigation. They left Mitchell's office feeling much better.

I should note, too, that the head of Mitchell's criminal division was Will Wilson, the former attorney general of Texas. As a Democrat, Wilson had been defeated for governor and U. S. senator, at which point he switched to the Republican party. In 1966 when I ran against Tower for the Senate, Wilson volunteered to be one of Tower's statewide campaign leaders. Tower later helped secure Wilson's job with Mitchell.

I felt that Wilson had held a grudge against me since I ran against him for attorney general in 1960, a race he won. After the race, I saw him at a chamber of commerce meeting in West Texas, and he made it clear to me that he did not appreciate some of the things I had said and done during the campaign; he grew very hostile. Later, when I was attorney general, he criticized me strongly because of a $100,000 settlement I had made in an antitrust case on the fixing of school bus prices, which he had filed before leaving office. He told others he felt I should have gotten much more. Also, after my losing race for the Senate, some of the Tower campaign files were turned over to me, and I found a memo from one of Tower's main men saying Wilson was being very helpful to them.

It seemed in 1971 that my biggest sin was being a past leader of the Democratic party in Texas. Although I had not held office for five years, nor was I particularly close to Barnes or a political threat to Tower, the decision apparently had been made that I was to be one of the "dead bodies" over which certain people would climb to success. It didn't matter that I was innocent.

I had not been wholly unaware of the investigation that had been quietly going on into the activities of individuals and corporations with whom I had business associations—such as Frank Sharp, John Osorio, Joseph Novotny, Michael Ling, National Bankers Life, Sharpstown State Bank, South Atlantic Corp. and RIC International Industries, Inc.

The SEC had directed me to appear at their Fort Worth regional office on December 9, 1970, and to bring all my business records.

The three SEC lawyers who took my deposition were strangers to me. We sat around a big conference table in a very stark, rather bizarre room. They obviously had already made up their minds. I felt that there would be no such thing as a fair hearing before these people. They grabbed my records, for example, and devoured them with their eyes as if they were starving and the records were food. When they mentioned the names of Democrats, they were mean about it. One of my interrogators, Steve Watson, slung a document across the table at me and demanded, "For the record, state the political position in the state Democratic party held by Dr. Elmer Baum."[1] I was stunned by the apparent venom in how he did that.

I thought, however, I had established beyond any doubt that I had never personally nor knowingly dealt in unregistered stocks, had no knowledge of the inside management or operations of NBL, had only the slightest acquaintance with Frank Sharp, and was completely ignorant of and uninvolved in any scheme or conspiracy.

The investigators were going down roads that to me were utterly ridiculous and unbelievable. If anybody was going to be hurt, it wasn't going to be me. If I had been concerned, I certainly would not have called my group together in January to make political plans.

How naive I was. The three weeks from the filing of the SEC complaint to the hearing for preliminary injunction on February 8, 1971, were a nightmare, a hell on earth for me and my family, with the baying of Republican politicians who scented Democratic blood, sensational and often distorted news stories and the whole uproar over the "stock scandals." My law practice dried up, and I had to dissolve my law firm, but the hardest of all to bear was the cool and questioning looks from many whom I had long considered friends. Others told me they were afraid to call for fear my phone was tapped. I was a shocked and lonesome man.

The press described me at first as "unperturbed" and "unruffled," but I was mightily perturbed and mightily ruffled.

In an interview with Dick Morehead of The Dallas *Morning News*, I dropped the pretense of calmness and lashed back at my critics and persecutors, telling them they could "go to hell—I've done nothing wrong."

Within days of the filing of the SEC complaint, however, Representative A. S. "Sid" Bowers, a Houston Republican, demanded that I be dismissed as chairman of the Speaker's statewide "Committee of 100," which had made recommendations for raising ethical standards in the Texas House. "It is inconceivable," Bowers yelped on the House floor, "that the man chairing the committee to study the ethics of the House should be involved in the current investigations by the SEC." Apart from the fact that the SEC charges had not been proved and it had not been established that I had violated any standards of ethics, Bowers's demand was a little late. The committee had completed its work and dissolved three weeks before!

Another Republican, national committeeman Peter O'Donnell of Dallas, called on Governor Smith to withdraw my appointment as a regent at Texas Tech, apparently not knowing that I had already been confirmed by the Senate 18 months before. Moreover, Tech regent chairman Frank Junell made a special trip to Austin to urge me not to resign. I remained on the board until my term expired in 1973.

The state GOP chairman, George Willeford, and Republican House members from Houston called for an investigation by the legislature, punishment for the wrongdoers and banishment of any guilty officeholders.

The SEC was only trying to prohibit me and the other defendants from violating the Securities Act. It was not asking for damages, and it was not seeking prison terms. This was a civil—not a criminal—case, but the way it was blown up and distorted in some news accounts you would have thought we were all headed for the penitentiary, if not the electric chair.

Still, the SEC did a very unusual thing. Prior to the hearing in February, it filed all of its depositions and documents with the court, which made them public. This meant my lawyers would have to compete with the press to read them, because the material could not be taken out of the courthouse.

The SEC apparently was trying to convict me in the eyes of the public through the press. I am convinced that the decision to smear and ruin me was reached at the highest levels of the Nixon administration, because I had had the temerity to challenge Tower and Wilson, because of speculation that I might run again, and because headlines disgracing my name—widely known throughout the state—would help Republican election efforts in 1972.

I have been told by friends that when they called on Tower in Washington, as late as 1971, he made it a point to remind them that they had supported me in 1966. They say an elephant never forgets, and this seems particularly true of the GOP elephant.

What Tower thought of me, however, was not nearly as important as securing a lawyer during those frantic, nightmarish weeks. After Barefoot told me he would not be able to stay on my case, I went to quite a few other lawyers without success, mainly because things were moving so rapidly that none had the time to add my business on top of what he already had. Also, SEC law is a complicated, specialized field and very few lawyers are qualified to practice it. Finally, with considerable discouragement and dismay, I called Leon Jaworski of Houston, a lawyer friend, and I asked Leon if he had any suggestions. He made one or two suggestions, one of whom was Charles Storey of Dallas, and I was able to secure him. He is one of the state's top lawyers and the son of Colonel Robert Storey, former president of the American Bar and dean emeritus of the law school at Southern Methodist University. At my request, while I was attorney general, Colonel Storey, together with Jaworski, had become one of my special counsels in the Texas investigation of the assassination of President Kennedy.

Charles assigned two of his associates, Paul Adams, Jr.—a staunch Republican—and John DeLay, to help him. The SEC had notified the 28 defendants that its volumes of depositions could be read at the SEC office in Fort Worth or in Judge Hughes's court. If we wanted our own copies, we could buy photo reproductions from a Dallas firm that was charging $4,000 to $5,000. I could not afford that expense. I wanted to save money by reading the depositions myself, but I hardly relished doing so in the office of the SEC "enemy." That left the judge's chambers, but this was where the press congregated. I knew I couldn't concentrate with the press firing questions and cartoonists sketching me. My only alternative was to send a lawyer to the judge's chambers and pay him his regular hourly fee.

He reported back almost immediately, however, that the situation was impossible. Depositions were piled all over the room and reporters, three and four deep, were scrambling for each new one fed to them by the SEC. He said after he located one of the more important depositions and had begun to read, a reporter asked him which one he had. Another reporter grabbed it, saying he was on deadline.

I appealed to the judge to require the SEC to furnish copies of the depositions, but she refused. I was caught between a hungry press and a federal agency wanting publicity. The rights of a private citizen under such circumstances aren't worth a plugged nickel.

We were being thrust into the courtroom blind.

3

"And Now as to Waggoner Carr"

On that bitterly cold morning of February 8, from Charles Storey's law office on the 41st floor of the Republic Bank Tower, I could see the old Dallas federal courthouse across the street. Word had gotten to us while we were making last-minute preparations for the hearing that there was quite a crowd over there, and Storey, DeLay and Adams had gone on ahead.

I stood at the window and looked down, feeling very lonely. I didn't know what was ahead, but I knew that the next few hours could be critical in my life, and I gave myself a little pep talk.

I put on my overcoat and picked up my briefcase and walked over. The press seemed to think I was the star of the proceedings, and they gave me special attention in that the cameramen met me before I crossed the street, backing in front of me and taking pictures as I walked. They did the same thing when I left the courthouse. This went on for three days.

In the federal building, reporters descended on me as guards made a routine inspection of my briefcase and while I was waiting for the elevator. I had to shove through a tumultuous crowd of reporters in the hall to get into Judge Hughes's small courtroom. It was so packed that some of the defendants' lawyers had to fill the jury box. We were lined up shoulder-to-shoulder in two rows in front of the judge's bench and, with the reporters and all, there must not have been more than five or six seats for public spectators. Many were turned away.

When the hearing opened, 17 of the 28 defendants, which included 15 individuals and 13 corporations, already had agreed

Photo: Clint Grant, The Dallas *Morning News*

GUARDS WAIT TO INSPECT WAGGONER CARR'S BRIEFCASE IN THE FEDERAL COURTHOUSE AT DALLAS BEFORE HIS FIRST HEARING IN THE SUIT FILED BY THE U. S. SECURITIES AND EXCHANGE COMMISSION.

to a preliminary injunction by entering a consent decree, and three had agreed to accept a permanent injunction. Only five individuals, including myself, were fighting a preliminary injunction. It would have been easier and cheaper to merely enter the consent decree, which is not an admission of guilt but simply a promise not to break the law in the future. My feeling was if I hadn't been beating my wife in the past, why sign an agreement not to beat her in the future. I was determined not to create the impression of guilt by meekly agreeing under government pressure to be law-abiding from now on.

I had to fight the case all the way in the courts, regardless of expense, embarrassment, damage to my reputation and loss of income.

I had suggested to Storey that since neither of us could see far enough ahead to figure out what type of legal job it was going to be, that he forego setting a price on his services and we'd just see what it came to at the end. He said he appreciated my attitude. I was very pleased with Charles. He was a conscientious fellow and really treated me with great respect.

SEC lawyer Robert Watson opened the hearing by offering in evidence 38 depositions which, with other documents, he said, supported the government's contention that the defendants had dealt in unregistered securities and otherwise violated the Securities Act. Watson rested the SEC case for the time being.

Charles Storey called me as the first witness, and I was on the stand for most of the day. At least one reporter wrote that I was calm and cool, and I may have appeared so, but inside I was churning. I was angry because they were trying to ruin me. I was the goat. They were charging me with things I had not done, and I had difficulty suppressing my emotions. Here was this great agency of government, with all its resources and power, throwing up a smoke screen to obscure truth and deny justice.

On the stand, I denied emphatically that I had ever traded in unregistered stocks or knowingly participated in any scheme or conspiracy to manipulate stocks. I admitted that I had owned shares in South Atlantic Corp. (SAC) and Nashwood Corp. and had been chairman of the board of City Bank & Trust, a small Dallas bank. I acknowledged that I was one of the owners of RIC

International Industries, Inc., a small conglomerate that was not a defendant. It had been put into receivership after Frank Sharp took it over in 1970.

I was one of six owners of Nashwood with 15 percent of the shares. It was a holding company, and I had been a director until I resigned in 1969. I also testified that I had bought 200 shares of Master Control, Inc., another defendant. I bought the stock for $14.50 a share—or a total of $2,900—and I still have it. It is absolutely worthless; you couldn't sell it, you couldn't give it away. Yet the SEC had accused me of having schemed to enrich myself there.

Although my former law partner, John Osorio, had been president of National Bankers Life, I told the court I had never participated in its management or operations, and he had never discussed them with me. In fact, I had never owned but 100 shares of NBL stock, which I bought in the early 1960s—when former Governor Allan Shivers owned the company—and I sold it in 1963. I made a profit, nothing sizeable.

I also testified that I had met Sharp, the alleged kingpin of the conspiracy, only twice in my life. Once was when we were waiting in line at a Braniff ticket counter in San Antonio and the other time was when we had lunch in Houston and discussed for two or three hours the possibility of RIC buying a high-rise apartment building which was owned by his Oak Forest Realty Co. The deal never came off.

My first ray of hope came when Judge Hughes asked the SEC lawyers during recess in her chambers what their contention was with respect to me. I was not there, but my lawyers told me that Robert Watson replied that the SEC was not contending that I had personally dealt in unregistered stock or taken part in the "scheme" in my "own name," but that I had done so through Nashwood and SAC and associates in other companies.

This was a startling admission by the SEC, and Storey quickly pointed it out. "This is not what the complaint says. Waggoner Carr is sued as an individual. It is alleged that Waggoner Carr sold unregistered securities, and that he participated in this buyer 'scheme.' It does not say that he did this in a derivative capacity or as an alter ego," Storey said. "If this complaint is to say that Waggoner Carr is in this suit only as the alter ego of a corporate entity, I would like very much to have the complaint amended." The judge merely said the private discussion had been helpful.

This private admission by the SEC that it had no evidence of my alleged personal wrongdoings did not stop the agency in the months ahead from feeding the news media statements that I had personally done something wrong.

During the hearing, Watson tried to tie me into a scheme to force up the market price of NBL stock, and I replied, "I never had any interest in NBL, and it would not have made any difference to me if the stock went up or down as far as my personal investments are concerned."

On the third day, after all the evidence had been submitted, Judge Hughes gave her ruling by reading from a paper she had prepared. She issued preliminary injunctions against Osorio and several others.

My pulse was pounding as she laid aside the first paper, picked up another and said gravely, "And now as to Waggoner Carr." It seemed to me that her voice got louder, and I couldn't imagine that tone carried anything but bad tidings for me.

She said I had been "intimately involved in a financial empire linked" to Sharp, but the "SEC has failed to establish" that I had "personally sold or pledged unregistered stock" or "personally violated the fraud section."

"Injunction," she said, "is denied as to Waggoner Carr."

Later, Judge Hughes rebuked the SEC for the haphazard, catchall tactics it had employed in its complaint, pointing out that the government had brought suit against a number of defendants for a wide variety of acts and had "sought to paint them all with the same broad brush . . . in its rush to establish joint liability, it had failed to lay proper groundwork for its case."

She said she hoped the SEC would not repeat this error at the hearing for a permanent injunction, which she set for August 30.

I was jubilant. I had been exonerated in my first major confrontation with my accusers. Several of the other defendants and their lawyers congratulated me. I told the press I would meet them at the elevator downstairs to answer questions, but when I went to get on the elevator it was full, so I walked down the stairs. I came out behind the reporters and cameramen who, with bright lights on, were intent on watching the elevator door open. I tapped one of the reporters on the shoulder and said, "Here I am."

As I drove home to Austin with Ernestine, I thought I had been vindicated and could begin to take up the threads of my life once more.

I could hardly wait to read the newspaper at breakfast the next morning, thinking, "Here my folks will see that I was innocent." That hope dimmed, however, when I picked up The Austin *American-Statesman* and found the story buried inside, with front-page headlines claiming that Travis County attorney Ned Granger was going to investigate me for possible violations of the lobbyist registration law. I called Granger, who was in St. David's Hospital recuperating from a January 15 auto accident, and told him I would be available for questioning at any time. He said he had not initiated the story of the investigation, that it had been done by George Keumpel, a reporter for The *American-Statesman*, whose publisher, Dick Brown, was a well-known Republican. I called editor Sam Wood and said the matter had been handled unfairly, and he was rather curt with me, which was unusual since we had known each other a long time. He said Keumpel was so young that he couldn't possibly have been prejudiced in his motives. This was hard for me to believe, but I think Sam felt I was being ridiculous, and I didn't try to argue with him.

4

Good Bill

Although the SEC's complaint was voluminous, public outcry centered on the now notorious banking bills that the legislature had passed in special session in September 1969. Although Governor Smith vetoed the bills, the SEC charged that I and other defendants had sought to influence the passage and signing of the bills by bribing the governor and certain key legislators.

From the outset, the SEC and the news media distorted the real purpose of House Bill 72 and the more important measure, House Bill 73. The passage of the bills was portrayed as a scheme to allow Sharp's tottering Sharpstown State Bank to get out from under regulation by the Federal Deposit Insurance Corporation.

At that time, the FDIC insured deposits up to $15,000. The intent of HB 73 was to allow state and private banks to form non-profit corporations to insure deposits between $15,000 and $100,000 under the supervision of the State Banking Board. It would have benefited every bank in Texas, especially the smaller banks. It was calculated to draw into Texas banks millions of dollars in larger deposits from outside the state that would not be brought in because of the $15,000 limit. The SEC said since there was no law that required a bank to have FDIC insurance, with the bill, the full $100,000 could be written under the state plan. The SEC said it was a fraudulent attempt to let Sharp escape FDIC regulations. Well, if that was Sharp's idea, he didn't say anything to anybody about it. Eugene Palmer in my law office drew up the bill and he didn't intend for that to happen.

That's not the way John Osorio explained it to me, either, and I have studied it since then; it just wasn't in the picture to get free of the FDIC. Former Governor Allan Shivers, who was generally credited with convincing Governor Smith to veto the bills, stated in a deposition to the SEC on January 11, 1971, that the way he read the bill it would provide insurance in addition to, not in lieu of, FDIC insurance.

I believe Osorio told me later that the bill was his idea. He thought it would please Sharp, who was his boss, and when he took it to him, Sharp said, "That's great. Why don't you draw up something like that." Osorio told Palmer to draw up the bill. The thought was if we could get the insurance up to $100,000, where you could put larger deposits in a small bank and still have it insured, more of the money would be spread around the little banks instead of it all being concentrated in the big ones. I was chairman of a small Dallas bank, City Bank & Trust, and the idea seemed great, because all it was doing was equalizing the big banks and the little ones.

The emergency clause of HB 73 clearly stated the bill's purpose:

> The fact that depositors in banks of this state are limited in protection of insured deposits to the sum of $15,000 under federal law and the fact that such sum is totally inadequate in view of inflationary pressures of the economy, and the fact that the citizens of this state should be provided with a mechanism for protection of deposits in excess of $15,000, create an emergency and an imperative public necessity . . .

If there is anything darkly sinister in that, I fail to see it. I predict that some day this plan, or one similar to it, will become law, and I hope it does.

Although none of them were named as defendants in the SEC suit, Speaker Gus Mutscher, Representatives Tommy Shannon and Bill Heatly, Elmer Baum, Governor Smith and others were mentioned prominently in connection with the passage of the bills.[1] Almost unnoticed was a letter from Sharp to Mutscher, dated February 19, 1969, which said, in part: "This bill is predicated on the idea that the FDIC will have the first $15,000 and the state the $100,000 above that." For reasons known only to Sharp, and possibly the SEC and Justice Department, Sharp, after he made his immunity deal, changed his story and told SEC lawyers the bills were to allow him to escape FDIC regulations. The SEC adopted Sharp's new story, even though he admitted under oath that he had never read the bills as passed.

Almost a year and a half after the SEC had accepted Sharp's version, hook, line and sinker, and had whipped public opinion into a white heat, a calmer head, capitol correspondent Morehead of The Dallas *Morning News* wrote in June 1972:

> Although three Texans have been convicted and others ruined politically by the 'Sharpstown Bank' scandal, some knowledgeable lawyers still doubt that the offending legislation of 1969 is as bad as advertised by later investigation of promoter Frank Sharp's financial empire. The bills were explained as providing insurance up to $100,000 on state bank deposits. But there's an argument over whether the legislation would have exempted state banks from scrutiny by the Federal Deposit Insurance Corp. (as Sharp said he was trying to do) even if Governor Preston Smith hadn't vetoed the measures.

I was elated when I read the column, because that's exactly the way I felt about it.

My first acquaintance with the bills was late in the second special legislative session after they had passed the House, when Osorio came into my office and told me what the bills did. He asked me if I would go up on the hill and talk to any senators that might have questions. I said, "Why sure, it sounds good to me."

I was told, and had no reason to doubt, that the banking board, the finance commission, the state treasurer and the Texas Bankers Association knew of the bills and did not oppose them.

When Osorio and I went over to the Senate, it was near the end of the session, and any filibuster or "tag"[2] would defeat them. There was the usual frustration and tension that exists during the last hours of the legislature—everybody wanting

Waggoner Carr smiles at a Houston Gridiron dinner in 1967, with Ben Barnes on his left. Two years later, when Barnes was lieutenant governor, they visited about two banking bills that became part of the Sharpstown scandal.

Photo: Houston *Chronicle*

everything through and everybody angry at everybody else—and there was a running feud between Senators Bill Patman and Jack Strong, who was sponsoring the bills. Patman was threatening to stop anything that Jack Strong backed, but when Senator Charles Wilson took over the bills, Patman dropped his opposition.

Osorio and I also called on Lt. Governor Barnes. He was sitting behind his desk, and it was a very hurried meeting because Ben was always in a hurry, particularly in the latter hours of a session. He was a great traffic cop, with bills going here and there, as he tried to clear his docket and keep everything moving. I had the impression that he knew about the bills and that the problem was not what was in the bills, but whether he was running into trouble in getting the bills passed. It was strictly a parliamentary discussion. There was no discussion about what the bills did.

At the time, everybody was for the bills. They had no opposition at all except the personality conflict between the two senators. It (HB 73) was a good bill. It had nothing but goodness to it.

After we saw Barnes, I left the Capitol. I had been there about an hour.

I had not registered as a lobbyist because I was not required to do so under the law, nor would any other citizen have been required to under similar circumstances. I received no compensation for my efforts. I contacted the senators for my personal benefit as an investor in a small bank, and not for any other person's benefit. Finally, I did not spend any money or give anything of value in my brief effort to help along the legislation. The constitution protects the right of a citizen to petition his government under such circumstances.

Ernest Stromberger of The Dallas *Times Herald* wrote that I had taken advantage of "an escape clause in the law," as if I should not be allowed rights every other citizen has, and Keumpel continued to write headline stories about the "bizarre legislative trail" of the banking bills. Thanks to the SEC, it was easy and popular to kick Waggoner Carr around those days.

As for Granger's investigation of my "lobbying" activities, which he had announced in February 1971, he told the Austin *Times* in May of that year that the "investigation" was over and the case closed. "You could call it a dead end," the county attorney was quoted as saying. "I talked to Carr, and he said he was just talking to legislators in behalf of his own interests. Under the law, a man can do that without registering as a lobbyist." The Austin *American-Statesman*, which had carried the front-page banner story that I was to be investigated for illegal lobbying, never even mentioned that Granger had decided my lobbying was legal. To my knowledge, neither did any other major newspaper, radio or TV station in Texas.

So another SEC-inspired "investigation" aimed at Waggoner Carr was quietly laid to rest three-and-a-half months later, with only a small, weekly newspaper to write its obituary.

5

Some Kind of Deal

Even after Judge Hughes stated from the bench in February 1971 that the SEC had not produced sufficient evidence to implicate me in any illegalities, the agency's attempts to drag me into the case at any cost continued; in fact, they increased. I felt as if the SEC was pulling out all the stops. Another lawyer, Lawrence Kiser of Washington, was sent to Texas to spend full time on the "Carr investigation," which several lawyers in the SEC's Fort Worth office already were working on. Investigators from the FBI and Justice Department also were involved, all acting under orders from Washington.

I submitted numerous questions to the SEC under the federal rules of civil procedure to force the agency to state what they were charging that I, personally, had done wrong. They refused to answer most of the questions because, they said, the answers would give me more information than I was entitled to before the trial, and also because they had not finished getting the information I had requested. As far as I was concerned, the SEC had charged me in January with doing many bad things and was admitting in March it had no proof. I was more convinced than ever that the SEC was relying on "trial by news media" and "guilt by association."

Effectively timed news releases began to appear, and the SEC dribbled out 60 more depositions, some of which were from second interviews with persons who might be involved in the suit. The stage was being set for my public execution. In March, Washington columnist Clark Mollenhoff wrote a column commending the SEC for investigations which, Mollenhoff said, "turned the heat on top political figures in . . . Texas, Arkansas, Louisiana, Ohio and Washington." He specifically mentioned that I was one of the original 28 defendants in Texas. The SEC obviously had conveniently neglected to tell Mollenhoff that the previous month it had failed miserably in Judge Hughes's court to prove any wrongdoing on my part. I wrote a letter to the editor of The Dallas *Morning News*—the first such letter I had ever written—and said, "One of the most un-American facets of our American way of life is our trial by news media." Would it have been asking too much, I asked, for Mollenhoff to have recited Judge Hughes's decision? "The most valuable thing to any man is his good name and reputation," I wrote the editor. "When those are under attack by others whose motives are undetermined, an honorable man will fight back with everything he has, even letters."

A lawyer for one of the other defendants returned from a trip to the Fort Worth SEC office and told me that Robert Watson had prominently displayed the Mollenhoff column on the office bulletin board. I got a prompt reply from The Dallas *Morning News* to my letter stating that the executive editor had given instructions that Judge Hughes's ruling be added to the Mollenhoff column, but the ruling had inadvertently been left out. The *Morning News* apologized and published my letter.

Almost like a two-pronged military attack, comments also were coming from the U. S. attorney in Houston, Anthony J. P. Farris, that a federal grand jury was investigating the so-called stock fraud case. One headline read, "Jurors Dig Deeper Into Fraud," which to me meant that, without benefit of a trial, the press was using the word "fraud" as a proven fact. The press coverage gave Farris statewide publicity, and the Houston press said he had strong ambitions to be governor.

At the same time I was squaring off against government attorneys, private lawyers in Texas were nipping at me. Two suits were filed against me, totaling $315,000, for allegedly trying to defraud banks in Houston and Lake Jackson by causing them to loan $105,000 to a man I had never heard of. I knew nothing of the loans and had never heard of the banks. I asked Storey to contact the law firm that was suing me, Geary, Brice, Barron and Stahl of Dallas, and I was particularly disappointed when Storey told me that Joe Geary, the lead attorney in the firm, a person I thought until then was a friend, had declined to discuss the case.

Several efforts were made to get me to settle out-of-court, and I repeatedly refused. I told one of the Geary associates, David Crump, I did not have the money, that I had absolutely no knowledge of the loans and I was not going to surrender to the public charges of fraud and conspiracy. On the day the trial was to begin, however, knowing it would cost up to $10,000 that I didn't have to defend myself, I felt I had no practical alternative except to accept a settlement they proposed. First Bank of Houston agreed to settle its $225,000 claim for $700, and the First National Bank of Lake Jackson agreed to settle its $90,000 claim for $300. Each bank told me I could pay them over five years, with no interest.

I insisted on a statement in the settlement agreement that I was still denying and protesting the allegations and was paying off only because of the great expense a trial would cost me. The banks and their lawyers agreed to the statement. The banks, in turn, required me to sign a provision releasing them from any claims I might have against them arising out of the lawsuit. Such a provision would block me, of course, from filing a suit accusing them of malicious prosecution. Again, I had to sign or face the unbearable expense of a trial.

On August 24, 1971, Judge Hughes signed an order dismissing the suits.

All the while, the SEC was throwing out hints that I could avoid trouble, embarrassment and crushing expense by entering a "consent decree"—a tacit admission of guilt. I thought their tactics bordered on blackmail, and I'll give an example.

One of my lawyers, Paul Adams Jr., told me that SEC lawyer Steve Watson had asked him why I would not enter a consent decree—without admitting any liability—and issue a press release in cooperation with the SEC reiterating that I had done nothing wrong. If I entered the consent, I could avoid the trial. Adams said he told Watson that the idea was repugnant to me, and I insisted on completely vindicating and clearing my name. Adams said that Watson then told him that the decision had been made, apparently by persons above Watson in the government in

Houston businessman Frank Sharp is shown in 1971 after he had testified before a federal grand jury in Houston. Sharp testified after pleading guilty to two minor violations and was granted immunity from further state or federal prosecution.

Photo: Houston *Chronicle*

Washington, that the government would appeal to higher courts if I were not enjoined. Watson reminded Adams what it would cost for an individual to fight the government on appeal. I knew the cost: at least $50,000 according to Charles Storey's estimate. There's no doubt that the government, which is so wasteful, would have spent much more than that on the appeal—all to get me. I asked Adams how he had replied to Watson. Adams said he informed Watson that I would defend the case to the hilt, and the threat of a government appeal didn't frighten us a bit. In fact, Adams said, we would appeal ourselves if I were enjoined. I told Adams, "You're 100 percent right. That's exactly the way I feel, and I don't want to give in under any circumstances."

On June 14, 1971, Farris filed an application in federal court in Houston to grant Frank Sharp immunity from prosecution. The application to Judge John Singleton specified that Richard Kleindienst, deputy attorney general of the United States, had approved the request.

Sharp came into court the same day, virtually without public notice, and pleaded guilty to two minor federal violations of making false entries in Sharpstown Bank books and selling unregistered stocks. Sharp was fined $5,000, which he paid with crisp $100 bills, and assessed a three-year probated sentence. In the judge's private chambers, Farris recommended that Singleton grant Sharp immunity from further state or federal prosecution, and Singleton did, except for possible perjury or contempt violations. Sharp went immediately to testify before the federal grand jury in Houston, sealing the bargain.

In one of 29 speeches he was to make from the House floor on Sharpstown, Congressman Henry B. Gonzalez of San Antonio said the Sharp deal "confirms my thesis that there is a vendetta by the Justice Department against Texas Democrats."

"The big one," Gonzalez said, "got away. The people will never know what happened at Sharpstown, or why. Justice is the loser, and the Justice Department lost deliberately . . . . This is a political case through and through."

State Securities Commissioner Truman Holladay said the immunity given Sharp "completely wrecks" possible state criminal cases pending against Sharp. Holladay said Farris had never consulted with him about the immunity deal, and the first he heard of it was on the radio. James Sims, the attorney in charge of the SEC Houston office, told reporters the Justice Department had negotiated the deal "behind our backs." After these remarks, he was suspended by the SEC for several weeks. Houston *Post* columnist Lynn Ashby apparently was the first to speculate in print that the Justice Department seemed more interested in torpedoing the Texas Democratic party than in justice. A person could get 30 years in prison for selling a single marijuana cigarette, Ashby wrote, but Sharp wouldn't miss a single day playing golf.

Sharp testified before other grand juries in Houston, Austin and Dallas and the Texas House General Investigating Committee, but The *Texas Observer* reported that Kleindienst "was none too happy with Sharp's information." It said Sharp had been "willing to provide titillating hearsay about politicians, but when asked specific questions, his arthritis was liable to start bothering him." The *Texas Observer* said Theo Pinson III of Washington had been told to take over the Houston investigation. Three other Justice Department lawyers were helping him—Charles Ruff, Robert Serino and Ralph Erickson. Farris was ordered off the investigation.

What did Sharp promise in exchange for immunity? He says he promised only to tell the truth. I don't know, and we may never know.

I know, however, that much later Ruff, Frank McCown, and others tried to make an "immunity" deal with Osorio. The proposed deal was that if Osorio would tell the "truth" and say he had bribed Ben Barnes to secure passage of the banking bills and had improperly influenced Governor Smith to appoint Elmer Baum to the banking board, they would not indict Osorio anymore. I do know about this proposed deal because Osorio told me, sitting in his apartment in Dallas, and in the second place it's in sworn court testimony. After they made the offer, Osorio said, he went to Austin to get Shivers's advice, and he went back and told them no deal.[1] I remember things were getting mean at that time; the government was playing for keeps, and I wasn't surprised at all that they had done something like that. As a matter of fact, I was kind of happy, because now it would come out publicly that they had tried to make a deal. Osorio told me that the Justice Department lawyers told him they didn't believe his previous statement to them, and he said, "Well, I have told you the truth and it is the truth." And they said they still didn't believe him, but they made it clear to him that if he would testify to these certain points they were not going to indict him anymore.

In thinking of why the Justice Department might have made an immunity deal with Sharp, I recall a story told me by Tim Timmins, a former assistant U. S. attorney who was representing one of the SEC defendants. After Sharp had been given immunity, he gave the SEC a deposition in Houston, and it was there that Sharp told about a purported conversation in which Osorio had supposedly said Barnes had performed well on the banking bills and was smart in that he only took cash. Before the deposition was completed, the testimony about Barnes had been leaked to the press and printed. As Timmins and Sharp's lawyer, Morton Susman, were leaving the federal courthouse, they noticed a headline in the afternoon paper relating the testimony. Timmins said Susman turned to him, smiled, and said, "Now, you know how we got Sharp his immunity."

Waggoner Carr speaks to reporters in Dallas after federal judge Sarah Hughes placed him under permanent injunction in an alleged stock manipulation scheme.

6

Rushing to Judgment

The path to my first big trial was paved with newspaper headlines. Even when the story was about another, I got the headline, such as this one: "Carr's Partner To Be Examined in SEC Fraud." Statewide publicity was even given to my second appearance before the Houston grand jury.

I have no way of knowing how many such stories appeared in Texas newspapers prior to the trial of the SEC civil suit, but I have reliable figures on the federal Northern Judicial District of Texas, which runs from east of Dallas to Lubbock and Amarillo. I collected the figures through the Texas Press Association clipping service, which I first subscribed to when I was Speaker in 1957-61. I was told that I had taken the service longer than anyone.

From January, when the SEC suit was filed, until August 30, 1971, when the trial began, my name appeared in 322 headlines, compared with 173 for Sharp and 80 for Osorio. In newspapers in that judicial district, my name appeared 3,928 times. I know, because I counted one day when I had nothing else to do.

Obviously, I was getting more than my fair share of headlines; even if my name wasn't mentioned until the 14th paragraph, I was in the headline. I was the fresh meat the feds were after.

In that same January 18-August 30 period, there were approximately 64,528 television newscasts throughout the state and 1,255,128 radio broadcasts, mentioning my name and

33

stating the latest SEC and Justice Department charges of law violations.

I got tired of listening to news broadcasts and tired of reading the newspapers. I felt as if I had been set up for the kill.

As I walked a couple of blocks from the downtown Holiday Inn in Dallas to the new federal courthouse on August 30, I realized I was facing the greatest crisis in my life up to that time. I had beaten the massive and powerful forces of the federal government in February; they could not afford to lose to me again. I had the inner strength of a man who knows he is right, but since January I had often been depressed, pulling from my billfold numerous times a poem which somehow inspired me. It was a poem by an unknown author that I had clipped from a publication put out by the Civil Defense Division of the Texas Department of Public Safety. I guess I had been on their mailing list since I was attorney general, and I still get the publication.

The last verse of the poem reads:
>Success is failure inside out—
>The silver tint of the clouds of doubt,
>And you never can tell how close you are,
>It may be near when it seems afar;
>So stick to the fight when you're hardest hit—
>It's when things seem worst that you musn't quit.

I read it again that morning, hoping to offset the cold and foreboding feeling I had in Judge Hughes's new courtroom.

The press sat in the jury box throughout the trial. The judge alone was to decide this case. Four SEC lawyers conducted the government's case. Several others kept track of documents and records that were being introduced, and at least two Justice Department lawyers from Washington sat in the audience making notes to consult with the other government lawyers at the end of each day.

Judge Hughes seemed impatient to get the trial over.

Sharp's lawyer announced that Sharp would accept whatever ruling the judge handed down, so she said there was no necessity for Sharp to be in the courtroom every day. I was required to be there, however, since I was contesting the government's case. While the government was putting on its case, Judge Hughes would tell lawyers, "Let's hurry, let's hurry," or "that doesn't have anything to do with this case." Many of the government's 69 witnesses were eliminated at the judge's urging. As a reporter for The Dallas *Morning News* noted, she chastised lawyers at the end of the first day's session by saying she could have summed up one witness's lengthy testimony in five minutes. The witness had been on the stand five hours. I felt at first her insistence on moving the trial along rapidly was good for me. As the trial developed, however, I thought she was simply rushing to judgment.

Defense lawyers became nervous about asking questions because she would say, "You ask too many questions" or "that's not a good question." Her decisions were snappy and curt. I like judges to be business-like, but not to the extent that it stifles the defense.

She also was getting elderly and had stated in a press interview that this was the largest and most involved case she had ever tried. I had the idea she was traveling down a road she had never traveled, and she wanted to get through with it.

A Houston *Post* reporter wrote that I was the "picture of confidence and prosperity" as I rocked in my chair, but he added that I was not rocking out of "boredom or bravado" but because my back hurt. I had been totally disabled by a pinched nerve in my back a few months earlier and had had to wear a very strong corset. The rocking was good therapy and it helped me relieve tension during the trial.

The government had gone into more detail since February, but a Dallas *Morning News* reporter noted the absence of "juicy revelations involving high political figures. It had been heralded that heads would roll, indictments be handed down and general calamity ensue. But not so." The SEC had used the news media so effectively prior to the trial that expectations were high, but I didn't feel the government was showing any more in September than it had in February that I had knowingly participated in an illegal scheme. I thought Sharp had, in effect, cleared me when he testified that we had met only one or two times.

Judge Hughes shook me, however, in ruling on a defense motion involving an SEC news release. The attorney asked the judge to delay her ruling until the release could be brought into the courtroom, and the following exchange took place:

> Hughes—I am familiar with the news release. I read it. It was a quote from Mr. Boltz?
>
> Attorney—That's correct, Your Honor.
>
> Hughes—I think I am sufficiently familiar with it that you can make your motion.

He stated his motion, and the judge promptly overruled it. The fact that she was familiar with the SEC release indicated that she had read, and perhaps studied, evidence outside the record, which is something that judges are not supposed to do. Her remark hit me like a fish in the face.

Later, she announced that defense counsel should cut their final arguments short because she already had substantially written her judgment climaxing the two-and-a-half week trial. Her judgment placed me, and the other defendants, under a permanent injunction. It said I had aided and abetted a stock manipulation scheme. I knew I was innocent. What had gone wrong?

I was near tears as I told reporters of my plans to appeal. The ruling completely crushed me. There weren't tears on my cheeks, and I don't remember any handkerchief wiping, but I remember how hard it was for me to talk and answer questions in the bright TV lights. It wouldn't have taken much for me to bawl.

My lawyers were in a state of shock themselves; Storey was speechless. He was as bad off as I was. I asked him later what he did, and he said he went home, got in his swimming pool and tried to relax. I think he took some days off.

"I know I'm not guilty," I told reporters. "As long as we know we're right, we'll fight this to the very end."

Judge Hughes's decision carried the law further than it had ever been carried before by holding that the pledging of unregistered stock at a bank to secure a loan was equivalent to a sale.

"If this is the law," I told a reporter a few weeks later, "every bank in Texas has violated the law, and is violating it now." There was no finding by the court that I was a principal in any of the things that she said were wrong. Because of my position on a board of directors or my ownership of stocks in some firms mentioned in the lawsuit—because of these, being in that position or owning that stock—I was held accountable for the actions of others, whether I knew about those actions or whether I did not, and the testimony showed that I did not.

Following the trial, SEC administrator Gerald Boltz said it had proved, "No political party is immune from corruption." His words in a moment of unguarded jubilation reinforced my belief that the SEC considered the suit as political, aimed at the Democratic party in Texas. I was nothing more than a sacrificial lamb. Within a few days, Boltz was promoted.

Reeling, but still on my feet, I returned home to Austin and became sort of a recluse. I didn't have anything to do. I didn't have a law office except a temporary setup with Les Proctor and Bob Jones, and I didn't have any clients. I had lost all of my business, all of my law practice, all of my estate. I didn't know how I would earn a living or how I would pay my debts. I had a heavy legal fee that I couldn't pay, and various lawsuits around the state that included me as a defendant added up to something in excess of $60 million. I didn't have anything really to make me get out and walk down the street. It seemed that everybody was looking at me and talking behind my back.

Although the SEC had dug my grave, I refused to lie down. I reflected that my inspirational poem said, "Rest if you must, but don't quit." I was only resting. Letters of encouragement helped, particularly a short handwritten note from Mrs. T. R. Simpson, an Odessa junior high school teacher, who wrote, "Our family has always had the greatest respect and admiration for you. We hope that you will continue to be a proud Texan and stand tall." She enclosed a one dollar bill. Coming at a time when I was shell-shocked, her letter was extremely touching and had a profoundly good effect on my morale.

I still have the dollar, as well as the letter, and I'm going to frame them and put them on my office wall at home.

Frank Sharp was the subject of a $100 million damage suit filed by Waggoner Carr. The suit is still pending.

7

My Appeal Fails

Immediately after the SEC trial, U. S. District Attorney Eldon Mahon announced that the Justice Department would, as a result of the hearing, search for possible criminal wrongdoings. "Our work," he said, "has just begun. Within the near future, we'll get the reports from the SEC and we'll take it from there." Like an echo, Boltz of the SEC Fort Worth office told the press, "We do have statutory authority to investigate these cases for possible criminal violations. We are going to do that."

Comments were coming out of Houston about possible grand jury indictments, and I had no doubt this case was going to be the most over-investigated one in history. For over a year the SEC, FBI, IRS, Justice Department and three grand juries had investigated it. I couldn't believe I would really be indicted.

So, I concentrated on my appeal of Judge Hughes's decision. The problem was I couldn't afford to appeal. The Storey law firm had charged me $50,000 in attorney fees for the SEC trial, and I couldn't pay that yet. Just to print the 3,000 pages of trial testimony for the appeals judges to read would cost $8,000, and I would have thousands of dollars in additional legal fees.

In late 1971 and into the spring of 1972 while I was sharing space with Proctor and Jones, I had a very meager business. I only made $7,091 in 1971 and $8,147 in 1972, and civil suits filed against me were taking up more and more time.[1] To appeal a decision I felt was wrong seemed a luxury I couldn't afford. The Fifth Circuit Court of Appeals, however, allowed me to forego certain expenses, and Storey appealed the decision in oral arguments in New Orleans without charging me.

On April 18, 1973, the appeals court affirmed Judge Hughes's ruling, 2-1, with the dissenting judge, James Coleman, stating that he had "serious doubt" whether the findings of the trial court justified the injunction. He said he would have directed Judge Hughes to dissolve my injunction. I would have felt better about the appeal if I had had adequate financing; we were skimping, and you never really know how much effect that has on a judge. I wish I could have put on a first class act, so to speak. This ended the SEC civil case on which the federal agency had spent hundreds of thousands of tax dollars for a trial conducted in the white heat of publicity and prejudice.

Long before that final decision came down, however, the federal district attorneys were stringing out press statements about possible indictments, which kept the "scandal" alive through the 1972 presidential elections.

I instructed Storey in October 1971 to write Mahon that we would appreciate being advised if any matter relating to me was presented to his grand jury. He said he would do so. Publicity against me by that time had become so one-sided, however, that when the president of a small defunct airline (Sentinel) was enjoined in connection with the sale and purchase of the corporate stock, the news stories featured the fact that the president was the son of the sister of Waggoner Carr's stepmother-in-law. Mrs. H. C. Story of Austin, my stepmother-in-law, took her first prominent mention in the newspapers in 40 years with good humor.

In December 1971—three days before Christmas—I filed a $100 million damage suit against Sharp, claiming, in effect, that he had ruined my reputation by concealing stock manipulations from me for which I had to answer. The case is still on file.

In the spring of 1972, Texas voters reacted as one might suspect to the unprecedented barrage of publicity, removing even honest public servants from office in the name of "good government." The political careers of Preston Smith, Ben Barnes and other Democrats were crushed, shattering any hope for statewide leadership in the 1972 presidential race.[2] The distrust that was sown in people's minds as to their state government was the most regretful result of this viciousness.

8

"The No. 1 Case in the Nation"

In April 1972 I had heard nothing from Storey in six months about an indictment, and since Mahon had promised to notify him if one were pending, I was beginning to relax. A Dallas *Morning News* story by Earl Golz—"Justice to Seek Carr Indictment"—splintered that calm. Golz's story said he had been told that the Justice Department would ask a federal grand jury to indict me by late May or early June, probably for mail fraud. He noted that the maximum penalty for mail fraud was five years and a $1,000 fine on each count.

I called Phil Warner of the Houston *Chronicle*, Ed Hunter of The Houston *Post*, Jim Maroney Jr. of The Dallas *Morning News*, George Johnson of The Dallas *Times Herald*, Jack Butler of the Fort Worth *Star-Telegram* and Richard Seaman of The Austin *American-Statesman*. I told them about Golz's article and said if they carried it, I would sue them. They said they appreciated my warning. Maroney said he hoped for my sake the story was wrong but for the *Morning News's* sake he hoped it proved to be accurate. Bonner McLane of Austin, who represented the Texas Radio and TV Association, advised me that the Associated Press had not picked up the story, but United Press International had used it. McLane said UPI told him that even if it were in error, I could not sue them because I was a public figure.

I reached Mahon at a convention in Atlanta, Georgia, and reported that McCown had been quoted in the article and that the story was certain to wipe out what little legal business I had left, as well as my reputation, and would destroy my unopposed campaign for state commander of the American Legion of Texas.[1]

Mahon sounded sympathetic and said he doubted that McCown was the source for the article, because he and McCown had not spoken about the grand jury investigation for a month. He remembered that I wanted to be told in advance if anything about me was to be presented to the grand jury. He said he would call me back, and he did the next day, reporting that McCown had told him he had never talked to Golz about me. Mahon said McCown had called Golz, and Golz said the information came from another source.

In one of my calls to newspapers, editor Charles Guy of the Lubbock *Avalanche-Journal* told me he had picked up talk in Washington that the Justice Department was going to ask the grand jury to indict me. He said he had run Golz's story because radio stations were blaring it out. It was consistent with the history of the whole matter that the news I was to be indicted would come out of Washington. It simply meant the signals were still being called from there.

Tom Geddes of UPI in Dallas called and said McCown had told UPI he did not know where the story came from, that it "certainly did not come from the Justice Department" and that no decision had been made "as to what would even be proposed in an indictment." I told Geddes I would sue anyone who carried the story. Geddes asked me if I would sue if UPI carried my remarks in the same story with Golz's article, and I told him that was UPI's risk, not mine. The UPI story only quoted me as saying, "This is a vicious and libelous story," eliminating the remainder of my statement.

In looking back, I must admit that Golz's and Guy's sources were accurate. In June 1972 McCown informed Timmins that I was going to be indicted and told him if I wanted to appear before the grand jury, I could request an appearance. Timmins relayed the message to me in Austin, but he was as mystified as I was why McCown had called him instead of my lawyer, Storey. Without telling Ernestine the disturbing news, I left early the next day for Fort Worth, where McCown outlined in detail what I would be indicted for—even before the grand jury voted. McCown and Mahon said the Justice Department was making all the decisions, and if I wanted time to collect evidence showing my innocence, I

Waggoner Carr, former attorney general, is photographed in Dallas after being indicted twice in 1972 for fraud and conspiracy.

should appeal to Washington. The Justice Department gave me a week to get my evidence to Washington over the protest of the SEC's Robert Watson, who said he didn't want any delays.

One week was totally inadequate, but my brother, Warlick, and I labored day and night in Timmins's office at the First National Bank in Dallas to meet the deadline. We used Timmins's Xerox machine, his library and his secretary, who typed our manuscript to send to Washington. Warlick had gotten involved after I told him I was going to be indicted. He was practicing civil law in Lubbock, but he spent hours helping me get together documents which turned out to be inches thick.

I also called Robert Pickrell, former attorney general of Arizona and a Republican, and asked him if he would talk to his friend, U. S. Attorney General Richard Kleindienst, who also was a member of the Republican party of Arizona. Timmins was a friend of Henry Petersen in the Justice Department, and he was going to contact him. I had met Pickrell when I was attorney general, and we had hit it off well. I didn't want special privileges, just a conscientious review by a person who wasn't prejudiced against me.

On the seventh day, Timmins and Pickrell took the documents and other evidence to Washington. They also carried a letter from Storey, which said, in part, "I deeply hope that, before any indictment is recommended against this man, a very careful review of these complex financial transactions will be made by one qualified and unbiased." Storey said he was convinced that I "did not knowingly participate in any scheme to defraud and certainly never held any criminal intent."

The same material that was turned over to Kleindienst was delivered to McCown who, without reading it, forwarded it to Lawrence Kiser of the SEC. Kiser had prosecuted the SEC civil action and was hardly the person I would want to review the material. He was convinced I had done all the things he had charged me with. Kleindienst gave the material to Robert Mahony of the Justice Department, who later told me he was already convinced that I was going to be indicted. I told McCown I was willing to go before the grand jury if he thought it would do any good, but I was under no illusions about my ability to dissuade the grand jury from indicting me if McCown wanted the jury to indict me. He nodded his head in agreement that the grand jury would do what he wanted them to do. I told him I would appreciate knowing in advance if I were to be indicted so I could get out of the Legion race. He told me I would be indicted.

Very shortly, Timmins and Pickrell reported my plea had been turned down. They were told by the Justice Department my case was on a "fast track," that I was going to be indicted and that my case was "the No. 1 case in the nation." I was dumfounded and overwhelmed. You've got the Mafia and the Ten Most Wanted Men in the nation, and yet my case was No. 1. It meant that it was highly important to someone that I be indicted, and that someone had to be in Washington. Whether it reached higher than the Justice Department, I didn't know, but to me it meant politics all the way through. It had to be important to hang my scalp on the wall.

Soon, Watergate would explode, and then what was happening in Texas would begin to make sense. I was part of a larger picture that I didn't really know anything about. The picture, however, included control of elections in pivotal states, including Texas, and to accomplish this, prominent Democrats had to be discredited.

On July 10, 1972, I was indicted twice, just as McCown had forecast. My indictments were perfectly timed. Texas was a "must" state for the Committee to Re-elect the President, and the election was just under four months away. One indictment alleged twelve counts to defraud National Bankers Life of $582,000 to pay personal debts. The second indictment of nine counts charged me, Osorio and four others with securities fraud, mail fraud, false filings with the SEC and conspiracy. To have gone so far to indict me, the Justice Department could now be expected to go all out to convict me.

The first thing I had to do was to get $3,500 to make bond to stay out of jail. Warlick borrowed it. A bank wouldn't loan me money. Next, I surrendered to the U. S. marshal at the federal courthouse in Dallas. I was mugged (photographed) with a number hung around my neck and fingerprinted. I was mortified, and Timmins was so embarrassed that he looked the other way.[2]

The federal magistrate, Patrick Mulloy, made it clear that I could not travel outside the state without his special permission. As I stood before Mulloy, the AP noted my attire: "He was wearing a pearl gray suit, pale blue tie with white shirt, and carried a straw hat with a wide blue and gold band." The whole proceeding almost destroyed my self respect. Kleindienst issued a three-page press release from Washington which his public relations people had prepared even before the grand jury returned the indictments. He later testified that such releases were issued out of Washington only in "selected" cases.

Seventeen days later, on July 27, 1972, I appeared in federal Judge William Taylor Jr.'s court for arraignment. There was a large crowd. I was last on the calendar and as I listened to the pleas of other defendants—on charges ranging from theft to violence—I observed that they were being released from custody without having to pay a cash bond. I asked my lawyer, Robert Travis, in a whisper why I was required to put up a bond, and he said it was because of politics. When my time came, Taylor asked if I understood the charges and that, if convicted, I could be sent to prison for 99 years and fined $95,000. I said I did. He asked for my plea, and I replied as firmly as I could, "I am not guilty, Your Honor." Whatever outward calm I showed was offset by the sick feeling in the pit of my stomach. I felt powerless; some powerful force was trying to put me in prison for 99 years.

On this occasion, to my relief, the press saved me the pain of reading what kind of clothes I had worn. Descriptions of my clothes irritated me because I thought there were more important things to talk about, and because it made me look like a fashion plate and gave me an image of being a show-off. The most serious thing I had to do was extricate myself and not worry about how my hair was combed or what suit I was wearing. The government was talking about me defrauding people out of millions of dollars, and all the reporters were saying was that I was dressed in million-dollar suits. I hadn't bought a new suit in three years and those I had bought came off the rack at places like Woolf Brothers in Dallas and Merritt Schaefer & Brown or Reynolds-Penland in Austin. Not only had I not bought a new suit for three years, I hadn't bought a new shirt, socks or even underwear—nothing. I couldn't afford to.

The overwhelming Texas vote for Nixon and Tower in November was depressing. Smith and Barnes had been soundly defeated in the spring, and Baum had resigned as chairman of the State Democratic Executive Committee. More Republicans than at any time since Reconstruction were elected to the Texas House and Senate.[3] There was no doubt in my mind that the large Republican vote totals had been substantially influenced by the GOP scheme to discredit Democrats.

During those unhappy days, I avoided contact with friends who were in such sensitive positions that they might be criticized for being seen with me. I had one heartwarming experience, however, which I must tell. In October 1972, approximately three months after I had been indicted, Ernestine and I attended the football game in Lubbock between Texas and Texas Tech. Since I was a Tech regent, we had special seats in the press box, which holds about 150 persons. Just before kickoff, it was disclosed that former President Lyndon Johnson also would be sitting in the press box. His seat was at the other end and, fearful that some photographer or writer might embarrass him by recording a greeting between us, Ernestine and I remained in our seats while others paid their respects. After the game had ended, as we waited to get on the elevator, we were asked to let Johnson's party go first. I avoided eye contact with him as he approached the elevator, but he astounded me by detouring to shake my hand and kiss Ernestine on the cheek. I was so shocked that I can't recall what he said.

Back in Austin, I wrote this letter:

Dear Mr. President:

Having the highest respect for you, I am convinced I should explain why I did not come by to express my good wishes to you while we both were watching the UT-TT game from the press box. This is the purpose of this letter.

Both Ernestine and I wanted to come by to visit. We discussed it. We, of course, realize we have a cloud hanging over us at this time. Fearful that some cameraman or reporter might use the incident to in some way embarrass you, we decided we should not. Thus, we gave up an opportunity to do something we wanted to do very badly.

We deeply appreciate your stopping to greet us on your way to the elevator. It was not only thoughtful but it cheered our night tremendously.

As a member of the Tech Board of Regents I thank you for coming. We hope you had a pleasant return to the ranch.

Yours truly,
Waggoner

His reply:

Dear Waggoner:

Thank you for your letter. I turned back at the elevator because I wanted you to know, and everyone else to know, that I was your friend, and I wanted to say so again to you and your dear wife. You have my understanding and my prayers.

Sincerely,
LBJ

9

"A Fool for a Client"

With a trial coming up and my personal resources depleted, I was having no luck obtaining a lawyer on a promise to pay. The law firm I wanted, Cantey and Hanger of Fort Worth, demanded $100,000.[1] I felt utterly helpless. That sum was way over my head. I was deeply disappointed in my own profession.

I asked Judge Taylor to move the trial from Dallas to another city in the northern district of Texas, preferably Lubbock. "A fair trial is all I want," I said at a pre-trial hearing December 13, 1972. "I want the federal government to prove its charges in court, not in the newspapers. I'm not sure I can get a fair trial, even in Lubbock, but I'm more likely to get an impartial jury in Lubbock than in Dallas." To illustrate the massive pre-trial publicity, I produced 4,000 newspaper and magazine clippings, nearly three-fourths of which had appeared in the Dallas-Fort Worth-Wichita Falls area. Taylor denied my motion, but he assured me that prospective jurors would be adequately examined.

My lawyers, Robert Travis of Cantey-Hanger and Timmins, then asked Taylor for permission to withdraw from the case because I could no longer pay them, and he granted the request. Travis had volunteered to work for free, but his firm insisted he not do so. Taylor asked if I wanted him to appoint a lawyer to represent me, and my reply was one rarely heard in our federal court system. "No, sir," I said. "I desire to represent myself."

My brother, Warlick; Travis Shelton, a Lubbock lawyer who would work with me; and lawyers in Dallas and Austin told me I

WAGGONER CARR (RIGHT) IS SHOWN IN DALLAS WITH TRAVIS SHELTON, A LUBBOCK LAWYER WHO HELPED IN CARR'S DEFENSE.

was making a bad mistake. They quoted what every lawyer has been taught: "A lawyer who represents himself has a fool for a client." I told Warlick, however, "Number one, I don't have the money to hire a qualified lawyer, Number two, I have full confidence in myself, and Number three, I want to do it. I'd just feel better if I do it—win, lose or draw." Warlick said, "Okay. I'm not a criminal lawyer so I don't know federal criminal procedure, but I'll help you." He suggested we get Shelton to sit in the "second seat" because he was an expert in procedure and criminal law. Shelton, later the president of the State Bar of Texas, and I had known each other since I had gotten out of law school. He lived in Tahoka, 30 miles south of Lubbock, and I hired him in 1948 as my assistant county attorney. We worked in Lubbock for about a year, and then I ran for the state legislature, and he ran for district attorney. He's an excellent criminal lawyer.

An important factor in my decision to represent myself was a letter I had received from John O'Connell, a good friend and former attorney general of Washington. He had just recently undergone two heavily publicized trials as a near-victim of the Justice Department, and the Washington tactics against him were virtually the same that I was experiencing. Here's what he wrote:

> I mortgaged my house and when it appeared that even if I won I would have a monumental attorney's fee bill for a Pyrrhic victory, I decided to represent myself. My practice had come to a complete halt and it would require all of my time to do this. Years back I had tried many cases and I found I could still do it. Keep in mind the atmosphere of these trials was that of a public execution because of the pre-trial press. The atmosphere had to be evened. The juries had to know what I was and not what my image was. In my stance there were tremendous advantages in representing myself. The principal one was that I could personalize my defense and get myself across as a human being. It was exciting. It dealt momentum. I would never have been satisfied at this crucial time in my life to have left this task to someone else even if he were successful.

One of the most important things I had to do was not to lose faith in myself. Day after day of press sometimes made me think 'maybe I am guilty of something.' Another problem I had in the early stages was a fierce and abiding, almost murderous hatred. After a couple of hours of sleep I would wake up full of hate. I was able to recognize that such feelings were self destructive. Hatred really destroys the one who hates. I was able to expel such feelings and I am sure in the trials that this was evident in my demeanor.

I was deeply impressed. I, too, had tended to "lose faith" and had been filled with "fierce and abiding hatred," but I thought I had overcome it, and I realized I would never be satisfied at this crucial time in my life to leave my defense to anyone else. I felt, for the first time, a sense of direction and confidence in my ability to prove myself innocent.

Shortly after my decision to be my own lawyer, several lawyers, including some of my former assistant attorneys general and one lawyer I had never met—Bruce Baldwin of Dallas—offered to help, free of charge. I thanked them, but I had set my course. I would devote full time to preparing for my trial in March 1973. This "fool" was ready to fight.

10

There Always Was Tomorrow

When the trial opened, March 6, 1973, I felt well prepared, but I was apprehensive. Would it be possible, I wondered, to select jurors whose minds had not been poisoned by publicity?[1] Would I be able to detect prejudice in prospective jurors? Warlick and Travis Shelton assisted me.

The lawyers on the other side were McCown, Mahony and Kiser. Mahony and Kiser had been sent from Washington specially to try the case. Osorio and his lawyers, Emmett Colvin and Jerry Birdwell, both of Dallas, sat between us. I considered McCown a pretty good trial lawyer. He apparently was a hard worker, but he was loud, boisterous and abrasive. Mahony was likeable most of the time and an average trial lawyer. He was methodical and sort of quiet, although he lost his temper on several occasions. But he was a fellow I could have liked under other circumstances. Kiser was a young fellow and he was trying to produce for his elders. I tried to avoid him like a skunk. He would turn the most innocent testimony into an incriminating thing.

One of the most disturbing developments of the trial occurred at the first when Joe Novotny, the former president of the Sharpstown State Bank, made a deal with the prosecutors and pleaded guilty to one count of the indictment charging mail fraud. Other counts in Dallas and Houston were dismissed and, to me, this was too similar to the deal the Justice Department had made with Sharp. The timing of Novotny's plea concerned me because I feared a juror would reason, "If one defendant pleads guilty, aren't they all guilty?"[2] We asked Judge Taylor to delay the trial until the publicity surrounding Novotny's plea had died down, but he refused.

Taylor, however, fulfilled his pledge to examine prospective jurors closely. Colvin, then I, and lastly McCown, questioned them, in addition to the judge. The usual procedure in federal court is for the judge to do all the questioning. After the first phase of questioning, prospective jurors were sent outside and called back to the courtroom one at a time. Questions then were confined to whether the person was prejudiced against the defendants or had a pre-conceived opinion of guilt or innocence. Such a careful procedure convinced me that Taylor was doing everything he could to assure that I would have fair-minded jurors. The questioning of 52 prospective jurors took three days. Four were excused at our request because they admitted they had formed opinions about the case from what they had read and seen in news reports.

Once I asked prospective juror H. A. Shipley the usual question: "Mr. Shipley, do you believe in guilt by association?" Shipley replied, "Absolutely not, Mr. Carr. Just because a man's in a chicken house doesn't make him a chicken."

Taylor immediately declared a ten-minute recess for us to regain our composure. Shipley, incidentally, was struck from the list by the prosecutors.

Every person questioned had either read or heard about the case, but most professed not to remember many details. All of them knew my name, but when one prospective juror was asked if he knew Sharp, he replied, "Was he from Athens?"

Four men and eight women were selected for the jury, and I felt each was honest and sincere, but I had serious doubts that some of them could understand the complex financial transactions in the case. There were housewives, a technician, an apartment owner and realtor, a labor supervisor, a shop foreman, an assembly woman, a secretary and a sales clerk in a woman's department store. I worried that a juror who had no experience with securities or large bank loans would have a natural tendency to feel that such large amounts must involve something illegal.

Shelton had sought unsuccessfully to get my trial separated from that of Osorio, who had been convicted in Amarillo the month before and sentenced to three years in prison and fined $6,000 for allegedly embezzling $641,250 from NBL's pension fund to buy NBL stock for the fund.

Unlike the SEC civil suit, the trial attracted few of the public. The courtroom was consistently half empty, and most of the spectators were legal or business friends of mine or the other defendants, or law students taking notes.

It took the government five days to present its case, and I knew everything about each of its witnesses through months of preparation. I had a file on every witness, every question I wanted to ask him and every document I wanted to ask about. After court closed each day, we had the same routine: working on those files. Travis Shelton and I would have a cocktail, after which we'd go eat and then return to the hotel room, either the Holiday Inn downtown or on the Central Expressway. Although we would have liked to have talked and relaxed more, there always was tomorrow. We had to get ready for the witnesses the government was going to put up. Warlick doesn't like to quit at any time, however, and he'd usually go back to the hotel and order a sandwich in the room and work on what he thought we should do the next day; he was all business.

I felt at the end of five days I had been able to turn every government witness into a favorable witness for Waggoner Carr.

It was at this point that Osorio's lawyers filed a bombshell motion for acquittal. The motion told of the meeting several months before we were indicted where McCown and Charles Ruff, assistant attorney general from Washington,[3] and others had allegedly promised Osorio immunity from further prosecution if he would testify he had bribed Ben Barnes and influenced Governor Smith to appoint Elmer Baum to the state banking board.[4] After Osorio rejected the alleged offer, he was indicted three more times, including the indictment on which he was now being tried. Taylor was fearful that the news media would report the contents of the motion and he would be forced to lock up the jury, so he ordered all attorneys and defendants not to make any public comments about the motion. A copy of the motion, however, accidently was left on the counsel table while lawyers were conferring in the judge's chambers, and a Dallas

Morning News reporter read it. The judge found out and chatted privately with the reporter. I asked him what had happened, and the reporter replied, "He threatened to put me in jail."

Taylor overruled the motion for acquittal, stating it had come too late in the trial to be considered. He promised to make the motion public after the trial, and he did.

I hung on every word of Osorio's six-hour testimony, which one reporter described as detailing a "complex web of financial deals. Deals that would boggle the mind of the average person." The spectators thinned out, and at times several jurors appeared on the verge of falling asleep.

In my opening statement, in the third week, I told the jurors I expected the evidence to show a $550,000 loan in question was a good loan for the City Bank & Trust Co. of Dallas, and that all the interest had been paid until the time Novotny and Sharp took RIC's assets over and failed to pay the note. "The purchase of RIC was a personal investment for me," I said. "It was my first real entrance into the business world, and I did it largely on the advice and recommendation of my friend, John Osorio. At that time, it appeared to be a good investment. Hindsight shows it went sour." I also said that when Sharp and Novotny took over RIC and assumed the note, they refused to pay $45,000 owed my Austin law firm for legal services, forcing the firm to break up.

As my own attorney, I testified from notes for two hours. Ronald George of The Dallas *Morning News* reported that I had been waiting since July to tell my story, and I told it, "without a questioning attorney," speaking directly to the jury. McCown cross-examined me for the better part of two days; he was sarcastic and biting.

It was brought out that I had actually underestimated my net worth by $95,367 in my financial statement in connection with the loan. It should have been $1.7 million—more than enough to have paid the entire note if it had been my obligation to pay the note when it came due. "I made a bad investment, but I am not a criminal," I said. When McCown gave up on me, I felt he had been frustrated.

Other witnesses followed. Insurance man Lonnie Langston of Lubbock testified that at the time Sharp took over RIC, I was

Waggoner Carr hesitates before responding to a reporter's question at his 1973 trial in Dallas for fraud and conspiracy.

working with him to raise my personal life insurance to include enough to pay all my debts, including the $550,000 note, which I certainly would not have been doing if I was intent on defrauding NBL by having it pay the note. A former law associate in Austin, T. B. Wright, testified about my concern over the note and that I had told him I was going to have to work hard to pay it. He confirmed that the law firm had not been paid by RIC so RIC could pay other bills and this led to dissatisfaction among the lawyers and caused the firm to dissolve.

Several testified to my good reputation and character, including the president of the Cotton Bowl Association, Field Scovell; Dallas oil-businessman Travis Ward, who was helping my son pay his way through dental school; Robert Smith, the Travis County district attorney who prosecuted the Speaker Gus Mutscher bribery conspiracy trial that grew out of Sharpstown; law professor Albert P. Jones of the University of Texas; former dean Robert G. Storey of the Southern Methodist University Law School; and University of Houston law students Bill Green and Chris Hanger.

After that, I rested my case. The jury had heard 18 government witnesses and 17 defense witnesses. I was exhausted. I seldom get hoarse, even after speaking for prolonged periods, but I often get tense if my diaphragm muscles get tired and I start forcing air. This makes me weak and my voice sounds tired. It helps to be able to take a moment and lean back in a chair and relax. We used a podium during the trial and it helped to get up and down rather than sitting all the time.

After each side had closed, an event occurred that illustrated the tactics with which I had been faced. McCown, in cross-examination, had asked whether Osorio and I had ever paid the balance of the purchase price of RIC, implying that by not paying we had defrauded the bank which had made the loan. I said, "No." Unknown to me, McCown had a telegram from the seller of RIC releasing me and Osorio from liability on the balance of the purchase price. So he already knew when he asked the question that we were not obligated to pay the balance. When we learned of the telegram, I asked Taylor to present the document to the jury, and he did so. McCown's apparent effort to withhold favorable evidence had backfired; he had pie all over his face.

The judge called for final arguments to the jury. As I arose, I realized that—as Godfrey Anderson of the AP would report—I was making the "most important speech of my life." I began:

> Yesterday I sat in this courtroom and heard a man call me a criminal. He accused me of putting my hands in other people's pockets. He accused me of stealing.
>
> I have been through the jungles of politics and I walked through those jungles with prestige and honor, and I came out of it unblemished and unscarred. It's not a very easy thing to hear another man call you a criminal, but then I don't believe Mr. Mahony really believed all the things he told you, because I think Mr. Mahony is a gentleman and I think he is doing his job as best he knows how. Of course, this case is a little more serious to me. It's my future he's talking about. It's my judgments and actions of three and a half years ago he now condemns.
>
> I think it is reasonable for you to assume that the long arm of the federal government has had every agent, every lawyer and the best prosecutors investigating everything I have done in the past four years. What they have come up with is a series of acts and documents I signed, not secretly, but publicly. Then they have glued those acts that were totally legally done in totally good faith, glued them together with their own statements, unsupported by the witnesses they put on the stand themselves, and with a lot of fantastic imagination made them into a ball of wax they call criminal. Not in one instance have they given Waggoner Carr or John Osorio the benefit of having some good purpose. Every act, they said, was bad.
>
> I signed the agreement to purchase RIC. That's right, I did. I don't deny it. I did. Oh, today I wish I hadn't; my world has caved in. I wish I had never signed that agreement. If I were defrauding I wouldn't be where I am today, caved in. Let the people who made money be

tried. I thought it was a good investment at the time, or I wouldn't have obligated myself for a half million dollars. I was mistaken, but I am not a criminal.

Fate has placed you on this jury. You are going to be my judge. You promised me that you would not allow the news media reports to influence your decision, and that you would judge me on what you hear in this courtroom alone. You promised me that you would be as fair in judging me as you would expect me to be in judging you if I were sitting in the jury box and you were standing here, and I believe that. And I took you as a juror because I believed that.

You today are the most important people in the world to me. You decide my life. My prayer is, and the last words I will get to say to you are, I hope you will have the wisdom to see the truth and the courage to speak it. My life will literally stand still from this moment until you come back and say "Not guilty."

I was confident the jury would acquit me, and they did after deliberating only two hours and 50 minutes.[5] Taylor slowly read out "Not guilty" 24 times to each of the 12 counts against me and Osorio. Ernestine hugged me, and Osorio dashed outside to call his daughter, Mrs. Pat Nickles. The three government lawyers refused to comment and left the court.

The acquittal left a nine-count indictment alleging fraud in the sale of securities, mail fraud, conspiracy and filing of false reports still pending against us in the same court. Four other defendants were scheduled to appear with us.

"I must be realistic," I told reporters, "but I hope to get the rest of this behind me as soon as possible so as to return to a normal life."

11

A Close Family

In May 1973 Judge Taylor granted my motion to dismiss me from a federal civil suit filed by trustee John L. King of RIC International, in which King alleged that I had used $200,000 in RIC funds to pay personal debts.

Life wasn't normal, but it was better—in some ways. Our family, for example, had grown closer together. Our son, David, 24, turned out to be a real source of strength to me. He was in Baylor dental school at Dallas, and when I had to tell him that my law practice had been destroyed and I had no income other than a few residuals and I could no longer afford to help him with his college expenses, his reaction was, "Why worry about it? The main thing is for you to win this battle. Don't let my problems concern you." He got a second-hand machine that made plastic nameplates—such as you wear on your lapel at conventions—and he made those for the faculty and students and earned a little profit. His wife went to work for Blue Cross. He backed me up in everything and encouraged me when I came to Dallas. He wanted me to sit down and talk about the most recent trial developments in detail. He had me out at the school one time and introduced me to his classmates and faculty and obviously was very proud of the way I was putting up a fight.

Ernestine's initial reaction to the first suit, the SEC civil suit, had been one of shock, and that was complicated by the fact that she did not understand all of the things that were being said or the charges that were being made against me. I really don't think she realized how serious it was, but I don't think I did either at first. I don't know that I ever told her how long I might go to prison if I

Waggoner Carr again talks to the press in Dallas, after he was acquitted on a 12-count indictment alleging fraud and conspiracy. Behind Carr (left to right) are his wife, Ernestine; his daughter in law, Diana; and his son, David.

were convicted in one of the criminal trials. She didn't want to listen to the radio or television newscasts because I was always the lead story. She got to where she didn't want to read the newspapers. She also felt that some of her friends were neglecting her.

Invitations to social events didn't seem to come in like they had, and she talked to me several times about how difficult it was to live under that kind of shadow. I think it was much more difficult on her than it was on me, but she never at any time cried or whimpered or made me feel like she was an extra burden. She did just exactly the opposite which, frankly, was a pleasant surprise to me with what she was going through. She had faith in me and never ever complained or expressed any doubt about my honesty. She didn't hesitate to hunt a job. She hadn't worked in many years, and had no particular ability; her typing was rusty, but she practiced and got a job, applying her money to helping us live.

She knew what I had to do and she bore it well. She always wanted to be present at the trials and sat on the front seat of the spectators' section and listened very intently to much of the testimony, although I'm sure it was too complicated for her mind in a business way.

The only time I ever saw her explode in anger was when she heard a friend of ours had indicated that the friend thought I was guilty. Ernestine gave her a call and really chewed her out. She reacted very strongly and very defensively against that. It was much like politics: if you win, everybody loves you; if you lose, many of them go their way.

The pleasant surprise was the number of people who went out of their way to express confidence, who remained loyal, and who had no hesitancy in being seen in public with me or Ernestine. We found out we had many friends who would publicly stand up for us. Whether the charges were correct or not, they didn't believe them, because they knew me and they had faith and confidence in me.

On the other hand, there was a certain amount of withdrawing. I had expected my friends in politics to withdraw from me. Politicians, being the creatures they are, withdraw from anybody that has any possibility of trouble that might rub off on them. There was, however, a good bit of that among other acquaintances, too—a kind of second look.

One incident that still disgusts me occurred when I went to Houston searching for information on Watergate. I had heard that Bradford Cook, the head of the SEC, and some other of John Mitchell's people had come to Texas during goose hunting season, and I had a feeling that the trips might have had something to do with me. It was beginning to fit together, and I was trying to find the key. I understood that Zarko Franks, the city editor of the Houston *Chronicle*, had some information on this, and I made an appointment with Franks. I was a little late for the appointment because I had had to drive from Austin and I hit the 5 p. m. traffic in Houston. We were to meet at the club on the main floor of the Rice Hotel. I went in, saw he was visiting with four or five men, and went over to let him know that I had arrived and that I would appreciate getting to talk to him when he finished his meeting. He curtly introduced me to the men there and, as I was leaving to wait for him in another part of the club, one of the men said in a loud voice, "You don't need to talk to that son of a bitch. He's under indictment anyway." For the first time in my life, I almost turned back and went over and jumped him. After that remark, Franks decided he didn't have time for me that day. He wanted me to stay overnight and see him the next day. I did stay overnight, but I didn't speak to him the next day. I had no use for him.

12

Crack In The Door

Even without Franks's help, I decided that I had enough facts to ask Judge Taylor to dismiss the remaining indictment against me on the legal doctrine of selective prosecution, which is a very rare motion. I felt that I was a victim of a scheme to destroy past and present Democratic politicians in Texas to assure the re-election of President Nixon and other Republican candidates, such as Senator Tower.

I didn't have the money or staff to conduct a thorough investigation, but I thought I had uncovered enough evidence of scheming to get the federal court to issue subpoenas for Mitchell, Kleindienst, Will Wilson, Patrick Gray of the FBI, and others for cross-examination.

I knew the odds that the court would dismiss the indictment were heavily against me: no legal precedent could be found where a person accused of a felony had been allowed by a federal court to question the motives of the federal government by subpoenaing high government officials. The fact that no one in 200 years of federal court history had ever done what I was trying to do was sobering. It was a life and death issue; the possibility of 99 years imprisonment for me was a life or death matter. I was desperate for an audience. Only the "official" version had been heard.

My motion to dismiss the prosecution was filed on July 9, 1973, one day short of the first year anniversary of my indictment. I took the 24-page motion to Dick West, a friend of mine at The Dallas *Morning News,* and said, "I think you'll be interested in this." West, who was editorial director of the

JOHN OSORIO (FRONT) AND HIS LAWYER, EMMETT COLVIN, WAIT FOR THE ELEVATOR IN THE DALLAS FEDERAL COURTHOUSE. OSORIO TESTIFIED AT A 1973 HEARING THAT A GOVERNMENT PROSECUTOR TOLD HIM HE COULD ESCAPE MORE INDICTMENTS IF HE WOULD SAY HE HAD BRIBED BEN BARNES TO PASS TWO BANK DEPOSIT BILLS.

Morning News, devoted an entire column to the motion, asking, "Was the Sharpstown scandal the Watergate of Texas?"

Osorio filed a similar motion to dismiss the indictment on the grounds of politicalization of governmental agencies. Taylor set a hearing on our motions for July 26, 1973.

On that day, Mahony filed a motion to deny my motion. He argued that I had no right to question the government's motives, and that I was trying to use the courtroom for a "circus." He ridiculed me by charging that my real hangup was that my political career had been destroyed, and I wanted the court to restore it. I replied that the court was not obligated to guarantee the continuation of my political career, but it was obligated to guarantee my constitutional rights, which Washington had denied. If the court denied me the right to present proof of my allegations, I had no other place to go.

Mahony and McCown said they thought my motion was unbelievable, preposterous, and stupid. I thought my chances were less than even of getting any kind of hearing, primarily due to the fact that I was making very serious charges against the President, and no court had ever heard such charges.

Since there was no legal precedent to do what I wanted to do, Taylor was cautious, but he granted a preliminary hearing for August 6. I don't think he would have done that had it not been for Watergate, which made schemes such as I was talking about believable.

What Taylor was saying was, "Okay, I'll open a crack in the door for you. If you can satisfy me that what you say happened probably did happen, I will allow you a full hearing later at which time Mitchell, Kleindienst and others will be subpoenaed to answer." I was elated; I felt like shouting for joy. It had been utterly impossible up until that time to get any court to subpoena heads of governments — the king can do no wrong. It was a tremendous victory.'

Beginning August 6, for three and a half days I presented my case. The only allegation I left out was that similar schemes had been put into effect in other states. I felt I had abundant proof of this, but I didn't have enough money to pay for witnesses from those states to come to Dallas.

On the first day, Julian Zimmerman, campaign finance chairman for Tower, testified about the meeting on December 4, 1970, which he and Tower had had with Mitchell in Mitchell's office in Washington. Zimmerman had told me he had requested the meeting, and I catalogued it in my mind. I asked him later if he would come to Dallas and help me. His reaction was, "You're embarrassing me, but yes, I'll do it because it's the right thing to do." After it was over, I called Zimmerman and thanked him, and he said, "I appreciate your calling me, but I feel good because I did it. It was a manly thing to do and a right thing to do, so you needn't thank me." In the conversation with Mitchell, Zimmerman testified, the attorney general said that Tower should not worry about Barnes because an investigation in Texas would affect Texas politics.

Also brought out was that someone in Washington had ordered the original SEC suit filed the day of the Democratic "Victory Dinner" in Austin, and to meet the hasty deadline, Boltz of the Fort Worth SEC office and his staff had had to make numerous corrections in the complaint in longhand.

I alleged, too, that arrangements had been made to get statewide publicity on the suit even though it was filed just before the courthouse closed for the day. A tip that something big involving the SEC was going to happen sent Houston *Chronicle* reporter Fred Harper by the SEC Houston office, where he got a copy of the complaint. Earl Golz of The Dallas *Morning News* happened to be in the federal courthouse at Dallas when Robert and Steve Watson and another man filed the complaint. Golz asked Robert Watson for a copy, and Watson refused. As they were leaving, however, Steve Watson turned to Golz, winked, and placed a copy on the table.

One of the most damaging witnesses to the prosecution at the preliminary hearing was State Banking Commissioner Robert Stewart, who testified that he had tried to get the SEC to delay filing the suit. "I felt the publicity generated by the lawsuit could cause a panic situation," Stewart said. Quinton Thompson, regional director of the Federal Deposit Insurance Corporation, told Stewart of the complaint on January 17, 1971, and they spent the next day with Boltz and the Watsons in an attempt to convince the SEC to hold off. Stewart said his examiners had found the Sharpstown bank insolvent in November 1970, but assets held by Sharpstown Shopping Center were placed in the bank's name, making it solvent again. He said he and Thompson had been in daily contact with the bank since November 1970 and the depositors were protected. Stewart and Thompson told Boltz that if the suit were filed, at that time, with false statements about the bank's condition, a run on the bank by depositors would close it by the end of the month. "The things complained about were serious," Stewart said, "but we didn't feel they were so serious that the public's money was in danger." At 5 p.m., Boltz's phone rang, and Robert Watson, who had left the meeting and driven 30 miles to Dallas, advised Boltz the suit had been filed. Further talk was useless, Boltz said, and Stewart and Thompson left.

As they had warned, the SEC suit touched off a run on the bank, and $15 million in deposits were withdrawn within a week. The bank had to close, and depositors needlessly lost millions of dollars. "Anytime you have publicity like that it can wreck almost any bank in the state," Stewart testified. It was the defendants, including me, and Democrat leaders, however, who got the blame, not the SEC.[1]

The testimony of another witness, Timmins, supported the incident I related earlier regarding Ben Barnes's alleged involvement, and I think the testimony is so important it should be printed verbatim.

> Carr — Did you attend the deposition that the SEC took from Mr. Sharp in 1971?
>
> Timmins — Yes, I did.
>
> Carr — Did you hear the questions and answers of that deposition?
>
> Timmins — Yes, for five days.
>
> Carr — Mr. Timmins, do you recall Mr. Sharp, just before the recess on the fourth day, being asked by Mr. Sims of the SEC about his recollection as to a discussion relative to Mr. Ben Barnes that took place allegedly in the Shopping Center Mall of the Sharpstown State Bank?
>
> Timmins — I remember very vividly the testimony in Houston.

Carr — And you were present when that took place?

Timmins — I was.

Carr — The purpose of my asking you that is, the record indicates after that question was asked and the answer was given that the court was promptly recessed until the following day. Is that your recollection?

Timmins — Yes sir.

Carr — Well, following that exchange, did you have a discussion with the attorney for Mr. Sharp, Mr. Morton Susman?

Timmins — Yes, I did. I had a brief conversation with him.

Carr — Tell us where it took place.

Timmins — We went down on the elevator together and across the lobby in the Federal Building on Rusk Street in Houston, and were going out the glass doors departing the building, and Mr. Susman and I were walking along together. And, of course, the last testimony we had heard during the day was Mr. Sharp's testimony concerning the alleged conversation with Mr. Osorio concerning Ben Barnes.

Carr — Just tell me what you said to him and what he said to you.

Timmins — I said to Mr. Susman, 'What is he going to come up with next?' 'he' referring to Mr. Sharp, and the subject being the Ben Barnes matter. Mr. Susman replied to me, 'Now you know why we got immunity,' and that's all that was said.

It was only after Sharp was granted immunity, I tried to convince the judge, that he testified that the banking bills were intended to allow him to avoid FDIC regulation by substituting the state deposit insurance established by the bill. Such substitution was the key in the SEC complaint to make it look as if Sharp had attempted to bribe state officials. To support my charge that Sharp had changed his story, I introduced his letter to Speaker Gus Mutscher that the state insurance would be in addition to the FDIC insurance and a memo by FDIC examiner

Ted Bristol, which was prepared at Sharp's request, that pertained to additional insurance in excess of the FDIC limit. Excerpts from a deposition by the bill's author, Eugene Palmer, and the governor's message submitting the banking subject to the legislature also were introduced. The governor's message specified "additional insurance."

As I noted in my motion, "The deal with Sharp was made solely for the political impact his public statements would have," as Sharp was never called as a government witness at any of the trials.

On the second day of the hearing, Tom Max Thomas of my old law firm and also a defendant in my pending trial testified that he had been offered a deal by government lawyers if he would tell more about his association with me. Thomas said he went by invitation in March or April 1972 to McCown's office in Fort Worth and McCown and Kiser were there.

Thomas testified:

> ... the statement was made to me, and I recall by Mr. McCown, that they didn't believe I was telling the truth or all that I knew of your [Carr's] involvement in particular transactions.... The statement was made then that probably it would be advantageous for my recollection to be as good as it could be involving those transactions and your participation in them. I asked specifically how it would be advantageous to me. And the response I got was that if my recollection was such that I could offer testimony that they appeared to want, then I would be allowed to plead guilty to one count of a forthcoming indictment instead of facing multiple counts of an indictment. This is at a time when I was not under indictment, and had not appeared before any grand juries, or anything.
>
> Carr — Did they indicate to you that you were going to be indicted as a certainty if you didn't do what they wanted you to do to me?
>
> Thomas — There wasn't any doubt in my mind.

On cross-examination, Mahony asked Thomas, "Did anyone suggest or say or intimate that you should commit perjury in exchange for any kind of deal?"

"Sir, at that point," replied Thomas, "I had said I had revealed everything I knew. I had given depositions and I had testified in civil cases, and I was told I wasn't telling the truth and I wasn't telling everything and it would be advantageous to me if my memory was better. Now, I think I could draw that inference from that, yes sir."[2]

Osorio was challenged by McCown on cross-examination after Osorio testified that McCown had told him in April 1972 that he could escape more indictments if he would "cooperate" by admitting he had bribed Barnes to pass the bank deposit bills and had improperly influenced Governor Smith to appoint Elmer Baum to the State Banking Board. McCown denied that Osorio had "ever been asked to commit perjury." He said the prosecutors had just questioned areas where they thought Osorio "was lying." Osorio replied: "I knew what I was there for. I'm not that naive." The session, he said, "was a threat on my life."

Osorio's co-counsel, Jerry Birdwell, testified about a Sunday meeting he and the other co-counsel, Emmett Colvin, had had with John Dean at his home in Alexandria, Virginia, July 29, 1973. Dean, formerly Nixon's legal adviser, said he had accumulated a voluminous file on Sharp, Will Wilson, and Sharp's immunity that "could prove very embarrassing to the administration," Birdwell said. Dean told them, Birdwell said, that the file was left "under lock and key in the basement of the White House" when he was fired by Nixon. Dean also said, Birdwell said, that he had attended a briefing in the summer of 1971 at which the possible consequences of Sharp's immunity were discussed with Patrick Gray, acting director of the FBI, and Justice Department lawyers Ruff and Henry Petersen. Dean said, according to Birdwell, that a few weeks later he received a Sharpstown file from Gray at the instruction of Mitchell. Dean said in skimming the file he found mention of a business relationship between Sharp and Wilson, including low interest loans with no collateral to Wilson after he had become assistant U.S. attorney general. According to Dean, Birdwell recalled,

Mitchell said it was up to Gray to "fire" Wilson. Wilson resigned in October 1971.

On cross-examination, Mahony asked Birdwell why Dean did not tell the story in court himself. "Did you ask Mr. Dean to come here to testify?" Mahony asked. "No," Birdwell replied, "because Mr. Osorio could not afford to pay his expenses." Osorio had signed a pauper's oath and testified in support of the oath that he owned no property, no car, no foreign bank account, had millions of dollars of civil judgments against him, and his wife had divorced him. "I live off my friends — that's all I'm doing," said Osorio.

To prove my oft-made point that I was included in the SEC civil suit and subsequent indictments to generate massive publicity, I introduced into evidence 2,726 newspaper stories which contained 626 headlines mentioning my name, as well as lengthy stories in national publications such as the *Wall Street Journal, Life* and *Fortune* magazines. I testified that my investigation had revealed that between January 18, 1971, when the SEC suit was filed, and September 15, 1971, when it was tried, there had been approximately 64,588 television newscasts and 1,255,128 radio newscasts in Texas and my name had been mentioned in most of them. Even more crucial, however, was that from July 10, 1972, when I was indicted, through the November general elections, Texas newspapers carried at least 121 prominent stories, including 104 headlines displaying my name. You can see why I felt I was being used by Republican candidates throughout the state as an example of why Democrats should be removed from office.

The 1972 election results, I felt, had been substantially influenced by Mitchell, the Committee to Re-elect the President and a White House scheme to control local and federal elections. "Now that this illegal and unconstitutional use of government power has come to light, it becomes the duty of the court to protect the individual rights of Waggoner Carr guaranteed by the constitution and laws of the United States," I told the court. "To permit an indictment to stand when it is tainted with abuse of government power and self-serving political motives will eventually cause our system of government to 'self-destruct' and the Bill of Rights to become forever meaningless."

The prosecutors presented no government witnesses, apparently feeling confident that the judge wouldn't pay any attention to me. They were lying behind a log.

In his final plea, Colvin said, "Until the Nixon administration and John Mitchell came in, I never thought I'd see the uneven hand of the U.S. attorney's office in Texas. That's something new to me and I've been around a long time. But, then, the Watergate is new to me, too!"

Mahony argued that we were "obviously making an effort to ride the crest of the Watergate situation. They use the big lie technique. Scream loud enough and hope somebody will believe it." I pictured in my mind the hundreds of thousands of newspaper stories and radio and TV newscasts screaming to my fellow Texans the message from Washington that I was a criminal. Those who had screamed the big lie technique were now accusing me of doing it to them. I was disgusted.

To the obvious consternation of Mahony-McCown-Kiser, Judge Taylor said in view of what he had heard he would conduct a full hearing. He authorized subpoenas at government expense for Kleindienst, Petersen, Wilson, Ruff, Robert Watson, Sharp and Anthony J. P. Farris.[3] The judge also ordered the Justice Department to deliver to him its entire file on Sharpstown and the file Dean purportedly had left at the White House. He said he would review them privately before possibly turning a portion of the files over to defense attorneys.

He set the next hearing for September 18, about five weeks away.

His ruling was an electrifying thing. The prosecutors were stunned; they couldn't believe that I had accomplished the impossible. Washington couldn't believe that a little federal district judge in far-away Texas was going to call all of them down there at government expense.

"This is just what we wanted," I told a reporter. "Now we are prepared to proceed."

13

Will Wilson and a Few Files

We had to wait a little longer, however, as Taylor postponed the hearing from September 18 to October 2 at the request of Kleindienst, who wanted to make a trip to Europe on behalf of some clients.

Of apparent concern to the government was a syndicated column by Rowland Evans and Robert Novak, which theorized September 5 that "charges that the Nixon administration misused the judicial process to shatter the Texas Democratic establishment may soon be backed up in part by President Nixon's former law-and-order specialist: Will Wilson." The column noted that Wilson had been subpoenaed for the hearing and added that Wilson "feels he was pushed out of the Justice Department by Kleindienst and Petersen. He has said recently in private that officials in the Justice Department who engineered the political collapse of Texas Democratic leaders were the same men who got rid of Will Wilson. He had to go, he says privately, because of his association with Houston land developer Frank Sharp; otherwise, the government's charges would be undercut."

It was September 20 before Taylor finally received the files from the Justice Department, plus those that Dean had mentioned. The judge released them to me and the other defendants after screening them. He also issued a "protective order" instructing us how they were to be used. I thought it was unnecessarily restrictive. Each of us was given only one copy of the documents and none could be copied. Even if a document was introduced into evidence in open court, the government could seek restrictions against its use. Any document not in evidence at the conclusion of the hearing had to be returned to government attorneys.

Because Wilson had scheduled a vacation out of the country for October 2, his testimony was heard the same day we got the files, giving us virtually no time to prepare. Instead of the "voluminous" file which Dean had described to Birdwell, however, there were only two items in the file by the time it reached me — a Houston newspaper article about Wilson and an October 1, 1971, memo from Gray, who was then with the Justice Department. The memo advised Dean of a phone call Gray had had from Wilson four days before. The memo said:

> Mr. Wilson stated that he wanted to pass along another thought. He said that his thought concerned Waggoner Carr, and he was very careful to point out to me that he and Carr had been at odds for years and were, in fact, *open enemies.* Mr. Wilson stated that it was S.E.C. custom to come up with a large number of counts in an indictment, and he indicated that they would probably bring 40 to 50 counts in *their* indictment against Waggoner Carr.
>
> Mr. Wilson then stated that *from the President's standpoint,* some degree of temperance should be exercised and that the S.E.C. should not be permitted to bring an indictment against Carr *if* that indictment contains a large number of counts. He said that Carr had a large following in Texas who would be very angered if he were kicked in this manner while he was down so to speak, and that such a kicking would *harm the President.* He further added that this is a situation in which Sharp is *not* going to the penitentiary and if we hit Carr with a heavy hand his friends are really going *to be bitter toward the President.*
>
> In the discussion of this particular point, he again reiterated that with reference to Carr it would not be good to *put the President* in the posture of bringing a heavy-handed, multi-count indictment against Carr.

> In response to a question from me, he at first indicated that *when reporting this conversation* I should not indicate that I obtained the information from him, but as we discussed this particular point he agreed that the decision to attribute it to him or not was mine and that I should use my own judgment. (Italics mine—W.C.)

Dean, of course, was at the time special counsel to President Nixon, and I must point out that the memo was written even before the grand jury that indicted me had begun its investigation. Yet the memo is already indicating 40 to 50 counts in an indictment against me. Since I was identified in the memo only as "Waggoner Carr," it appears that my identity was well known in the Justice Department and White House even though I had never met Gray or Dean or anyone else in the White House. Wilson's advice — based solely on what was good or bad politically for Nixon — apparently was followed as I was indicted twice. The first indictment consisted of 12 counts and the second nine counts. This memo obviously reinforces my argument that the decision to indict me was made in Washington as part of a scheme to destroy the Texas Democratic Party prior to the 1972 national election.

Wilson was on the witness stand for two hours, and I asked him about the memo. He said he couldn't remember making the call to Gray.

He admitted, however, that he had conferred with Mitchell several times about the possibility that increasing publicity tying him to Sharp might embarrass the President. Wilson said at first Mitchell was sympathetic and had told him Nixon was, too. But the publicity became so embarrassing that Wilson was forced to resign in October 1971.

Somebody in Washington apparently was very nervous about what Wilson might say because several court reporters took down his testimony in relays. One court reporter said the testimony was being hastily transcribed so prosecutors could relay it immediately to Washington.

Tom Thomas subpoenaed Mitchell and Gray, and I subpoenaed Tower, after hearing that Tower had requested and

SENATOR JOHN TOWER (LEFT) AND ATTORNEY GENERAL JOHN MITCHELL STAND AT A DALLAS BANQUET. BOTH WERE SUBPOENAED TO APPEAR AT A 1973 HEARING IN CONNECTION WITH CARR'S ACCUSATIONS THAT HE WAS THE VICTIM OF A REPUBLICAN PLOT, BUT ONLY MITCHELL CAME. TOWER WAS EXCUSED BY A SENATE RESOLUTION.

received a complete file on Sharp and Sharpstown in 1971 before any criminal charges had been brought against me. I also had been advised that Mitchell's daily logs showed he had more contact with Tower than with any other senator. The subpoena was served on Tower in Washington, September 27, but he promptly got the Senate to pass a resolution prohibiting him from attending the hearing. Tower's lawyers in Dallas hurriedly filed a motion to excuse him based upon the resolution, stating that the five-day notice was insufficient for him to schedule a trip to Dallas and that he was chairman of the Republican Policy Committee, which had a meeting October 2. Furthermore, the motion said, Tower had none of the documents specified in the subpoena nor "has he ever had such, nor to his knowledge have such items ever existed."

Tower in his motion said he "would be willing to testify before the court at a time and date when the Senate is not sitting in session." This was estimated to be in December, three months after the hearing. He was excused. Within two weeks after the hearing, however, while the Senate was still in session, Tower came to Dallas for two speeches, including one to the Dallas-Fort Worth Chapter of the Association of Old Crows.

On September 22, based on the conversation Dean had had with Birdwell, Colvin and I filed motions asking the court to subpoena White House tapes of conversations that purportedly related to Sharpstown. We specifically requested the tape of a White House conversation July 29, 1971, between Nixon, Mitchell and Tower. Those tapes, Colvin said, are "obviously material to show that this present indictment is founded upon intentional discrimination for non-governmental purposes." Taylor denied the motions.

Further study of the files resulted in our issuing additional subpoenas, including those for:

— George Willeford of Austin, former chairman of the Texas Republican party. The Justice Department file revealed that on August 19, 1971, Willeford had encouraged Ruff over the phone to bring Barnes's name into the Sharpstown investigation. Willeford was quoted in Ruff's report as saying he "knew 'you guys' have been working hard and wouldn't it be nice if we could convince Osorio to bring Ben Barnes into the investigation."

— Richard Stakem Jr. of Austin, district director of the IRS. I subpoenaed him to get the IRS file on the income tax audit that started on me almost simultaneously with the filing of the SEC suit in January 1971. I couldn't help but laugh when the only records turned over to me were the annual returns that I had prepared and signed. Alton Franke, the examiner I had dealt with, had been pretty snotty, and perhaps it was mere coincidence, but after the subpoena was served on Stakem, his boss, Franke became very friendly. He complimented me, for example, on the records I kept and how cooperative I had been.

— Devan Shumway, director of public affairs for the Committee to Re-elect the President. The subpoena commanded him to bring committee records and correspondence with the SEC, IRS, FBI, Justice Department and the White House pertaining to me and Sharpstown. Shumway and his lawyers wired me on the opening day of the hearing that he had not been able to find any such documents and did not know of any. Since the committee had disbanded and, I was told, few of the records remained, I gave that inquiry up as a lost cause.

— Theo Pinson, former assistant U.S. attorney under Farris in Houston. Pinson was one of the attorneys sent from Washington by Kleindienst. He had investigated Sharp and recommended to Farris that Sharp be granted immunity in exchange for his testimony.

Also subpoenaed were McCown; former chairman Bradford Cook of the SEC; Novotny; general counsel Robert Clines of the Texas Insurance Department; and Nixon, or his authorized representative.

The federal marshal couldn't find Cook in time for the hearing. It was hard for me to believe a man of his prominence couldn't be located. Novotny apparently had moved from Houston, and his subpoena was never served. I had wanted Clines to testify about the January 18, 1971, meeting in Fort Worth of Boltz, Thompson of the FDIC, and Stewart, the banking commissioner, but Clines had just been released from the hospital and I excused him.

The subpoena for Nixon went unanswered. Not only was the subpoena apparently ignored, but we never got back the $325 we sent to pay Nixon's plane fare to Dallas. A tongue-in-cheek motion was filed later to get the money back, but the judge didn't do anything. The court, of course, couldn't begin to find $325 in the White House.

Of more concern to me were what I considered glaring deficiencies and missing documents in the Justice Department file. For example, some documents referred to attached exhibits, but the exhibits were not attached. At least one report stated it was the first of three, and the other two — apparently pertaining to Sharp's immunity — were gone. No SEC or Justice Department documents were included from September 1971 to September 1973, nor was there anything showing Justice Department activities from November 20, 1970, to May 24, 1971. You had detailed coverage of all developments from a certain date to a certain date, then you had a gap, like a gap in a tape, then six months later it would take up as a continuous saga. You knew there had been something happening during that period of time; as a matter of fact, it was during that period that the Justice Department was seeking the indictments against me. During that 1970-71 period was the SEC trial, and the Justice Department was sitting in on it, so to tell me that they didn't make reports to Washington on what was going on was ridiculous. How naive can you get? Were they just sitting around turning in expense reports? You know perfectly well they were making reports to Washington, but there was total silence as if the tape had been erased.

I never received a single item covering the two-year or six-month periods, nor did the prosecutors ever offer to explain their failure to provide them. I complained to the court about the obvious silence in the files, but I never got any results. Whether the file the judge got had documents covering that period of time I have no way of knowing, because I couldn't see what he was culling. But I have to believe if there had been anything in there that he felt was material to me, that he would have given it to me.

FORMER ATTORNEYS GENERAL RICHARD KLEINDIENST (TOP) AND JOHN MITCHELL (BOTTOM) ENTER THE DALLAS FEDERAL COURTHOUSE FOR THE "TRAVELING WATERGATE SHOW" IN OCTOBER 1973.

14

"The Traveling Watergate Show"

When the marshal called Judge Taylor's court to order October 2, 1973, he opened with a lengthy prayer — something he had not done previously. He, too, seemed impressed with the hearing. There had never been one quite like it. When the witnesses stood to be sworn, the line-up was a mixture of Watergate and Sharpstown personalities. The Dallas press named it "the traveling Watergate show."

There was a good bit of motion and commotion, with a standing-room-only crowd of spectators. The press sat in the jury box. A crowd of more than 250 gathered in the lobby each of the four days to get a glimpse of famous faces, such as Mitchell, but except for the first day, he slipped up the back elevator and out that way, too.

Kleindienst was the first witness, and the judge's restrictions on the use of government documents made it cumbersome to try to cross-examine him because we couldn't read from the documents. How in the world could I ask a question about a document without telling the witness what's in the document that I want to ask him a question about? Finally, after we piece-by-piece got questions pertaining to the documents asked and answered, I think it became obvious to the court that such protection was a sham. There wasn't anything left to protect. It was all out anyway. It was silly. So, he released the documents.

Colvin questioned Kleindienst first, giving me a chance to observe him. He was a good dresser and a glib talker, with a persuasive personality. His memory, however, was consistently bad on the detailed memos he had written. He testified that someone else had written them, and he had merely signed them. During Colvin's brief examination, Kleindienst responded 67 times with, "I don't recall," "I have no recollection," "My memory is very hazy on that," "I don't know," "I haven't the slightest idea," and "I'm not positive about that." I know it was 67 times because I got a transcript and counted.

Kleindienst also testified that Farris had called him long distance and recommended immunity from prosecution for Sharp, but he had refused to authorize immunity because he wanted the agreement a little more definite as to what Sharp was willing to say in return. After a second call in which Farris purportedly told Kleindienst he had tied down Sharp's testimony so that the Justice Department could prosecute him if he did not say what he had promised to say, Kleindienst testified that he approved the immunity. He told Colvin, however, he could not recall on what factors he based his judgment. Later, when Farris admitted to Kleindienst in a Washington taxicab that Sharp's testimony "with respect to other persons" had not been put in writing nor signed by Sharp, Kleindienst testified that he got very upset. He said Petersen was "as irritated as I was, if not more so. He didn't generally want to grant immunity anyway."

Kleindienst said he called Farris back to Washington July 30 and forced him to sign a letter asking to be relieved of the Sharpstown investigation "in view of the sensitivity and complexity" and the "manpower limitations of my office." The letter suggested that the Justice Department should supervise the investigation. Another letter from Kleindienst to Farris said, "I am . . . quite willing to agree to your suggestion," which, of course, was really Kleindienst's suggestion. Ruff was designated as the leader of a four-man team of lawyers, including Pinson, Ralph Erickson and Robert Serino. The letters were a perfect camouflage for Washington to take over the case, and they must have galled Farris.

When I questioned Kleindienst, his poor memory resulted in 66 responses such as "It could have been, but I don't recall," and "I don't recollect." As I returned to my seat I wondered how you prove something when the witness who should know can't remember.

Questioned later by David Gibson, the lawyer for another defendant, Kleindienst admitted he had understood that most, if not all, of the persons Sharp was to testify about to get immunity were elected Texas officials. He testified, however, that he called Mrs. Anne Armstrong of Texas, who was working for Nixon in the White House, and asked her to tell Republican officials in Texas not to contact the Justice Department about Sharp. His call, Kleindienst said, was prompted by Willeford's call to Ruff about Osorio and Barnes. Kleindienst remembered he made the Armstrong call "immediately after I received this information. It wasn't something I put off for an hour or a day, I did it immediately." This tended to show, of course, that the Justice Department had rebuffed Willeford's suggestion and kept the Sharp investigation free of politics. His memory was sharp in favorable areas.

Petersen was next up. He had been Wilson's deputy in the Justice Department, and when Wilson resigned, Petersen replaced him as head of the criminal division.

His memory was much better than Kleindienst's, and he appeared to be a candid, straight-forward man. He was a mixture of a bureaucrat who wanted to speak out and an employee of a political boss who had to watch his words and please his boss. I'd never seen a character of his type before. He was a pro.

Petersen testified that on the day immunity was approved for Sharp, Farris was talking long distance to Kleindienst while one of Farris's assistants was talking to Petersen, who said he opposed immunity. Petersen said he had never considered Sharp's offer of testimony to be detailed and definite enough to be useful. After Petersen had hung up, however, Kleindienst, whose office was two floors above, called Petersen and advised him he had approved the immunity.

This exchange took place while Petersen was on the stand:

> Carr—Well, then, reading between the lines on what you're saying, Mr. Petersen, wasn't it the failure of Mr. Farris to get the specifics from Mr. Sharp that you all were expecting up there relating to the Democratic politics or officials of Texas that resulted and triggered his removal?

Petersen—Mr. Carr, you might say that and I might say that and Mr. Farris would say something different, but in any event, I was not pleased with the manner in which the case was proceeding.

Carr—Then when the decision was made to remove Mr. Farris from all responsibilities in connection with the Sharp matter, in effect, the investigation and the supervision of it was moved directly to Washington, was it not?

Petersen—That's correct.

Petersen contended that since the federal team on the Sharpstown case consisted primarily of career lawyers, the investigation had no "sense of political motivation." He testified, "I don't think they are political eunuchs, but I do think as far as the selection process can guarantee it they were unbiased politically." Although he tried to paint a picture of a Justice Department that historically never lowered itself to thinking and acting politically, I didn't buy it.

One question Petersen refused to answer was whether he had told Kleindienst about the Justice Department's established guidelines for granting immunity—guidelines that Wilson had testified were not followed with Sharp. Petersen also refused to spell out the precise recommendation he made to Kleindienst.

When I asked if he knew why the announcement of my indictment was made from Washington, Petersen answered that it was because of the "large political connotation." He then turned me off by saying I would have to complain to someone else about that. His attitude was, I don't call those shots.

After he stepped down from the witness stand, Petersen walked over and shook the judge's hand. Taylor seemed surprised and, from the look on his face, apparently pleased. I thought it was a rather brazen act on behalf of Petersen. Taylor smiled and was cordial to him, and I didn't like it at all. It was completely out of place and was disturbing to me as a defendant for a partisan witness to go greet the judge in open court. You just don't do that.

As I questioned L. Patrick Gray III, I couldn't help but recall that he had already admitted to Senator Sam Ervin's committee that he had destroyed Watergate papers at the request of the White House. As a result of this, the Senate had refused to confirm him as the successor to J. Edgar Hoover as director of the FBI.

Gray appeared to be a kindly man, but I felt that his testimony and demeanor showed that he was obviously awed by famous names and men in authority. I'll cite one of his responses to illustrate this.

> Gray—Yes sir, I was ordered by the then attorney general of the United States, John Mitchell, to examine into the information and materials available at that time in the Department of Justice concerning the relationship between then Assistant Attorney General Will Wilson and Mr. Frank Sharp. That was my specific charter and order from the attorney general of the United States.

Remember, it was Gray who had written the October 1, 1971, memo reciting his phone conversation with Wilson about how my indictment should be handled. He was so precise that he recalled he had dictated the memo from "9 a.m. to 9:20 a.m." He showed it to Kleindienst, and perhaps Mitchell, and sent a copy to Dean. I asked him if Wilson had indicated how he knew the SEC would probably indict me on 40 or 50 counts, and Gray replied, "No sir, he did not."

Gray hardly seemed cut out to be part of the Nixon-Mitchell team. But he was beholden to those who brought him honor and prestige, even to destroying possibly incriminating evidence at the command of the White House. Yet, as the Watergate White House tapes revealed, Nixon criticized Gray because he had failed to control the FBI investigation of the cover-up.

Mitchell was the last witness before noon on the second day, October 3. To insulate him, besides bringing him up the back elevator, Mitchell's lunch was served in an off-limits area near the courtroom. His attorney, William Hundley of Washington, who had represented Mitchell when he testified before the Senate Watergate committee, was with him at all times. I had met Hundley when he was on Attorney General Robert Kennedy's staff and came to Beaumont, Texas, to speak. I introduced him.

On Mitchell's arrival, a reporter asked him in the lobby, "Will you take the fifth?" Mitchell replied, "A fifth of what? A fifth of Scotch?"

Before Mitchell testified, I had asked Hundley if he could arrange a meeting between us. It was an unusual request, but I wanted to meet Mitchell and tell him what I was interested in asking him so he would have time to refresh his memory. The meeting was set for 8:30 a.m. in the grand jury room next to the court, and Hundley excused himself.

Mitchell and I were left alone in the room, with his pipe, and his pipe was really the most active of the three of us; he was puffing on it pretty strongly. His hand, holding the pipe, quivered. Seeking desperately to make conversation, I said, "Mr. Mitchell, you've been leading a hell of a life lately, haven't you?" He sucked on his pipe a couple of times, withdrew it shakily from his mouth and replied, "Yes, yes, I certainly have. But that's the way life is. Up one day and down the next. A man just has to last it out. I'll do it." He puffed again, in silence, looked at me and asked, "Yours hasn't been too good, has it?" I responded, "No sir, it certainly hasn't," biting my tongue to keep from blaming him for my misery. Nevertheless, I was surprised at how comfortable the meeting was.

One of the telltale things that I noticed, although we'd never met, was that he called me Waggoner like an old friend. There was no doubt that somebody had been talking to him about me. He knew the path I had been over.

In court, Mitchell testified he had been an independent until 1966 when he registered as a Republican. He had practiced law in New York with Nixon, and Nixon had appointed him attorney general, a job he held from January 20, 1969, to March 1, 1972.

Questioned by Travis Shelton, Mitchell testified he had discussed with Nixon in the summer of 1971 the "prior connection" between Will Wilson and Sharp. He met again with the President on the same subject in early October, and Wilson resigned in mid-October.

> Shelton—And, sir, at the first meeting you had with the President, I believe you, both you and the President, expressed your confidence in

Mr. Wilson, did you not, and reached a decision to keep him on?

Mitchell—That was the decision that was reached . . .

Shelton—Yes sir, but then at the second meeting the decision was made that perhaps that he ought to be or that he should resign his position as assistant attorney general?

Mitchell—I think that's the general conclusion, yes.

He also testified that it had been brought to his attention that public officials and former public officials might be involved in Sharpstown. The names, he recalled, were Preston Smith, Gus Mutscher, Barnes and me. He said he knew they were all prominent Texas Democrats. Mitchell remembered, too, the meeting with Tower and Zimmerman, but he said he did not recall discussing an investigation that might remove Barnes as a potential opponent of Tower's. Hundley noted that the difficulty getting Mitchell's 1970 daily logs, which I wanted, was that they were in the New York apartment where Mrs. Mitchell was staying, and the Mitchells were separated. "He can't get in," Hundley explained.

I would have expected Mitchell to have been antagonistic toward me and the other defendants who had brought this hearing upon him, but he was kind of like an old shoe, an old Joe. He didn't seem to be tight, except when his hand shook. It seemed to be another day's chore for him, as if he were sitting among friends.

As he was leaving the courtroom to go back to New York, Mitchell bent over as he walked past the counsel table where I was sitting and whispered, "Good luck, Waggoner." I was so surprised that I smiled and could only reply, "Good luck, John."

I couldn't add it up, except that here was a guy who once was the hunter and now he was the hunted, and he has sympathy for anybody that's going through the same thing. He never did, however, send me a copy of his 1970 logs.

I thought Farris was the man in the middle. He was somewhat of a frustrated politician, having run for Congress and lost, and news reports had said that he had urged immunity for Sharp because Sharp promised to testify to things which could make Farris governor. On the stand, he appeared to be smoldering over Kleindienst's testimony blaming Farris for foulups in granting Sharp's immunity. He bristled at suggestions that he had been at fault in the matter. Kleindienst had laid it on him good, and it was obvious that he was using the knife to draw a little blood of his own. At no time, Farris said, had Kleindienst directed that Sharp's proffered testimony be reduced to writing or be given before a court reporter. This was in direct conflict with Kleindienst's testimony. He also disputed Kleindienst's testimony about the two letters concerning his resignation. He insisted that he was removed at his own request and wrote his own letter. I felt his pride was coloring his memory.

Farris testified that he had a dozen or more meetings with Sharp or his attorneys about what Sharp would trade for immunity, beginning in April 1971, but in the two meetings where Sharp was present my name was not mentioned. Sharp's lawyers, Morton Susman and Jerry Hill, brought my name up, Farris said, as one who had helped push the banking bills through the legislature, suggesting that Sharp would trade his testimony about that as well for immunity.

Farris testified, too, that Washington had approved a deal Novotny had made with McCown in which Novotny pleaded guilty to a minor charge and the remaining indictments were dismissed. Novotny was fined $1,000 on his guilty plea.

Several months after the hearing, Farris was quoted as saying Kleindienst's allegations about him had been "a lot of bull." With Tower's help he sought reappointment to another term as U. S. attorney for the Southern District of Texas, but Senator Lloyd Bentsen, a Texas Democrat, blocked the appointment because he objected to Farris's handling of Sharp's immunity. Told that the Senate would not confirm him again even with Tower's support, Farris resigned in August 1974.

Sharp placed the government's first contact with him or his attorneys much earlier than Farris had—as early as seven months before immunity was granted on June 14, 1971. He said he had many de-briefing sessions with government investigators.

Photo: Houston *Chronicle*

Former U. S. attorney Anthony J. P. Farris of Houston, who filed application in 1971 to grant Frank Sharp immunity from prosecution.

He recalled, for example, that a "Mr. Erickman" of the Justice Department had asked him if he would "like to meet Jerry Boltz." Sharp said he asked who Boltz was, and Erickman told him he was the top man for the SEC in Texas. "I said to him," Sharp testified, "that I didn't have too many years left on this earth, and I thought I could certainly get by the rest of my life without ever seeing or hearing from Mr. Boltz."

"And then," Sharp said, "he [Erickman] asked the question, 'Will you see Mr. Boltz?' And one of my attorneys said, 'Yes, Mr. Sharp will see Mr. Boltz.' So he [Boltz] came to Houston, to Jerry Hill's office, and it was a very sad occasion for me for this meeting, really."

Sharp said Boltz told him, "Mr. Sharp, I know you hate me for what has been done to you." Sharp said he replied, "Mr. Boltz, I do not hate any living soul in the world and that includes you, but, by this one act of yours in Dallas, you have destroyed what my life has been built on. Ever since I can remember and certainly ever since my wife and I have been married, we have tried to live a life that would be a credit to our children. You took that away from us. My net worth on my financial statements showed in excess of $30 million. You took all that away from me at one time, but I don't hate you."

Sharp was asked what he meant by "at one time," and he replied, "I meant when he [Boltz] filed the injunction up here in Dallas for the purpose of closing the bank and really putting me out of business."

Sharp testified that Boltz said, "We realize that we have done what you have said, but by us working and cooperating together, surely we can amend this and reverse what has been done." Sharp added, "He [Boltz] did say in conclusion that, 'We realized when this injunction was filed that it was going to close your businesses and probably several others, but the decision was made in the Washington office.' And I am still puzzled at this last remark. And he said there was one person that would not stop the closing—the injunction. Now, what that means I do not know . . ."

"In other words," Sharp was asked, "he never did mention who that one person was?" Sharp replied, "No sir, he did not."

I thought it was a rather amazing story; that was the first time it came out. Sharp had not told that story before.

Later, Colvin asked Sharp about his conversation with Osorio in which Barnes was mentioned. Sharp recalled that he and Osorio were sitting in Sharp's office at the Sharpstown State Bank in Houston and had walked into the foyer. Sharp quoted Osorio as saying, "Well, Ben did what he said he would do." Sharp said he replied, "Now are you telling me that I have a financial responsibility to Ben Barnes?" Osorio answered, according to Sharp, "No, no, no, you do not have."

Colvin asked if there had been any other conversation with Osorio, and Sharp said, "Not that I remember."

How dramatically different this was from Sharp's earlier story, when he quoted Osorio as saying, "Oh, no, no, I just—oh, no—I've already taken care of that. You know, Ben is smarter than most of these other politicians—he takes only cash."

Robert Watson was, I believe, the most stubborn man I've ever seen or known in my life. He would have made a great Prussian general. He was hostile, pompous, technical and so anxious to overwhelm everyone that he had to be admonished by the court not to make speeches but just answer questions.

Watson denied having a conference with Stewart, the banking commissioner, on January 18, 1971, in direct contradiction of Stewart's testimony, but he admitted that the SEC and Justice Department had been collaborating since November 1970 and that the SEC had referred the matters on which I was later indicted to Wilson. This differed from his previous testimony that after the 1971 trial the matter had been turned over to a grand jury.

Watson also said that no indictments had ever been brought in the 40 years the Securities Act had existed charging the pledging of securities as being a violation of the law, as it was charged in my case.

Watson made much of the fact that he and Boltz were career—not political—appointees. He did not mention that Boltz formerly was on the staff of William Saxbe when Saxbe, a Republican, was attorney general of Ohio. Saxbe later became U.S. attorney general in the Nixon administration.

Watson did admit he and Boltz had talked about how much publicity the SEC suit would get. Watson, obviously with his tongue jammed in his cheek, said he had predicted that the filing of the suit would be reported on either the business page or across from the classified ads. He said, however, he could not recall if there had been any handwritten corrections in the typewritten complaint—which might indicate it had been filed in haste. When I showed him a copy of the complaint, with more than 100 handwritten corrections, Watson admitted some corrections had been made but said he could not remember why they were made.

Before court adjourned October 5, 1973, Taylor refused to order Nixon to produce tapes of his conversation with Mitchell about Sharpstown. The judge said he would need ''some showing of inference'' of criminality on the part of the person who had the tapes before he could issue such an order. The tapes recorded conversations between Nixon and Mitchell. Since we could not subpoena Nixon, and Mitchell said he couldn't remember details of the conversations, we were unable to meet the burden of proof the judge required to get the tapes.

On January 16, 1974, Taylor denied our motions to dismiss the indictment and set my trial on the remaining indictment for February 21.

I was disappointed. I had obviously hoped that this might end it. To think about subjecting myself to another criminal trial was something less than a happy thought. But Taylor had certainly given me my ''day in court,'' and after I rationalized it, I realized that no one in 200 years had ever gotten as far as I had gotten. The fact that the judge had caused high officials of the federal government to come to Dallas was itself an historic event. I had gained an objective, and that was to lay out publicly the whole story of the political shenanigan proposition.

I had been able to show, through the press perhaps, that this was a phase of Watergate that had never been revealed in Washington.

The only disappointment, outside of the judge's decision of course, was that we were no match for them—Mitchell and his people—in the courtroom. They descended with their faulty memories and orchestrated answers, and we were not prepared to cope with that. What you would have to have is an investigating committee like Senator Ervin's. There is no way for a lone individual to get ready for experts like that. You're just pecking at the door; you're like a little dog chewing at their heels. If you asked a question and they said, "No," or "I don't remember," that was it. You had nothing you could throw at them. You knew the answer was somewhere, but you couldn't get to it.

There is such an iron curtain between an individual of this country and the government that the fight between the two is totally unfair. All the power, all the money, all the authority is on one side—the government side—and an individual is simply not armed for that kind of fight.

I now faced the final court battle, knowing that the "feds" would go all out. It was their last chance. It was my last chance to clear my name. I went back to work.

Photo: Houston *Chronicle*

Former Governor John Connally (left) wishes Waggoner Carr well after Carr had addressed thousands of supporters in a 1966 Austin campaign speech for the U. S. Senate.

15

An Honest Man

I felt completely alone in those months from October 1973, when the traveling Watergate show ended, to late February 1974, when my second trial on criminal charges began. I had no investigative staff, secretaries or expense account as the government did. It was up to me, and only me, to run down leads.

It cost me $195 just to get microfilms of documents, which the government had moved to Washington to make it more difficult for me. Fortunately, Warlick volunteered to help study them. We used the microfilm readers at the Dallas Public Library on Commerce Street.

I had borrowed some money from friends—I couldn't go to a bank—and one or two legal fees came in. I also sold an interest in an apartment house at Waco, and I had a $10,000 debenture. It seemed like everytime I was about to go under financially something would come up.

Since I had lost my law clients, I even closed the office I had at Les Proctor's and turned most of my equipment and furniture over to one of his associates. I took a desk home, however, although it was so big I had to move it through a window to get it into my house. I spent almost all of my time at home preparing for the trial. My greatest relaxation was my feeling of accomplishment in my defense. When I would work hard to get a pleading done or to get my evidence in shape, that would give me the relaxation I needed. Occasionally, friends in Dallas would take me fishing there or in East Texas.

In January, before the trial, McCown announced that he was replacing himself with a young, eager prosecutor, Richard

Stephens. He was tall, slender, cleancut and always courteous—if you could consider anyone who was trying to put you in the penitentiary as courteous. He was a pretty sharp boy, but he was obviously a beginner trying to earn his spurs. McCown said he had important matters in Amarillo, but the talk around the courthouse was that he thought it would be bad politics to be associated with another defeat. His departure still left Mahony and Mary Curtin of the Justice Department in attendance, as well as Stephens, and Kiser of the SEC. Four prosecutors were formidable enough.

I was following Watergate very closely because, with all the investigations and revelations such as the White House tapes, I felt there was a chance that something might be revealed that would be material to my defense. I ordered copies of the Ervin Committee's reports and contacted Senator Lloyd Bentsen's office; Robert Strauss and the Democratic National Committee; and Lyndon Johnson's former press man, George Christian. I was going in every direction trying to find out information in Washington.

Mahony and Curtin asked the judge to prohibit us from inquiring during the trial about matters concerning prosecution for political reasons in the presence of the jury. They also asked that no inquiry be allowed regarding Sharp's immunity; Wilson's resignation; Barnes; the role of Justice Department lawyers in the case; my prior acquittal; the Watergate matter; or any persons connected with the Watergate matter, including but not limited to the following:

> Anne Armstrong, J. Fred Buzhardt, Charles Colson, Committee to Re-elect the President, Bradford Cook, Archibald Cox, John Dean, the so-called Enemies List, John Erlichman, Anthony J. P. Farris, L. Patrick Gray, Robert Haldeman, Howard Hunt, Richard Kleindienst, Egil Krogh, Gordon Liddy, John Mitchell, Martha Mitchell, Richard Nixon, Henry Petersen, Eliott Richardson, William Ruckelshaus, Office of the Special Prosecutor, Maurice Stans, John Tower, and Dr. George Willeford.

One of the thrusts of their motion was that it would be prejudicial to them for the jury to know Mahony and Curtin were from the Justice Department or out of Washington. I told my associates it was a sorry state of affairs when Justice Department lawyers were fearful a jury would be prejudiced by the mere mention of the fact that they were from the nation's capital.

The judge overruled the motion except the request that no mention be made of the prior acquittal, which was proper.

The government lawyers then dropped all charges of mail fraud, which left me charged with fraud in the sale of securities, false filing with the SEC and conspiracy. The government also dismissed all charges against Jarrell Ormand and Tom Thomas, and they agreed to testify for the government. Mahony declined to give his reasons for dismissing the charges.

Jury selection began February 21, 1974, and the panel consisted of 62 persons. We questioned the panel as a group the first day and then began questioning the prospective jurors individually—an unusual procedure that the judge also had allowed in the first trial in an extreme effort to assure a fair-minded jury. The individual questioning was limited to finding out what effect, if any, pre-trial publicity had had on the prospective juror.

The prosecutors asked the court to disqualify one man who said he gambled four or five months a year and "possibly" might be sympathetic to others who were charged with breaking laws. Another was excused after he said he had been brought before a judge once on a misdemeanor charge and could not help but feel sorry for anybody brought before a judge. Several were excused because they felt the defendants had to show evidence that they were not guilty—in direct conflict with the law that a person is innocent until proven guilty. A policeman's wife ended up on the jury to the initial concern of some of the defendants after she said she was "independent minded" and would not be prejudiced because of her husband's profession.

Prosecutors asked if the fact that I was my own attorney would make a difference. All answered no.

An experience that made my day, however, was the questioning of Robert Lamon, a fellow about 35, who said he had

Photo: Lee Langum, The Dallas *Morning News*

WAGGONER CARR ARRIVES FOR HIS SECOND TRIAL IN DALLAS — IN 1974 — WITH ONE OF HIS LAWYERS, TRAVIS SHELTON (LEFT). HE WAS ACQUITTED OF ALL CHARGES.

followed news of the stock scandal closely and had even lost money that he had invested in National Bankers stock. I wanted to dismiss him as being prejudiced against the defense, but when one of the lawyers asked him if he were prejudiced and, if so, against whom, Lamon replied, "I feel very strongly that Mr. Carr is innocent. I think the government has framed him and he should not be here." Judge Taylor thanked him for being truthful and dismissed him. As he was leaving the courtroom, I couldn't resist saying, "And I thank you also, Mr. Lamon." He turned to face me, held up his hand with his thumb and forefinger forming a circle and responded, "Good luck, sir." After hearing nothing for days except the prosecutors' hostile words, Lamon's comments were like manna from heaven.

We finally secured a jury at the end of the fifth day. It included eight men and four women, including four blacks and a Mexican-American. Their occupations ranged from porter to electronic's technician to janitor, from bacon presser to sandwich maker, from warehouseman to the policeman's wife, certainly a cross-section of America. But they were strangers, and my fate was in their hands.

The clothes-conscious AP had noted I was wearing a "light grey suit," and the press once again referred to my "silver" hair. Frankly, I was tired of it. Much more of this, and they could truthfully change the word "silver" to "gray" or, possibly, "none."

This was inconsequential, however, compared with a statement by Thano Dameris, a Houston lawyer, which said, in part, that on July 8, 1970, he had flown to New York where he met with certain people "and possibly Waggoner Carr." I didn't even know the guy, but when Mahony gave me Demaris's statement it was like a great triumph. Mahony's attitude was, "There you are! How do you like that! I got you!" It was important for the government to establish that I was at the meeting, because bank loans were discussed which the government contended were fraudulent.

Since there was a good bit of camaraderie among the lawyers for the defendants, and hardly anything was a secret, I heard from them that prosecutors had questioned Dameris so intently he began to think I possibly could have been at the meeting and added that to his statement. To try to get statements, the prosecutors were pounding, "Waggoner Carr, Waggoner Carr, Waggoner Carr, what can you tell us about Waggoner Carr?" Through all of this, I learned that success in dealing with the prosecutors depended on what you could tell them about me. I was the big target.

When I cross-examined Dameris, the following exchange took place:

>Carr — You have testified that to your best recollection Waggoner Carr was in New York on July 8, 1970. Are you sure of this?
>
>Dameris — No.
>
>Carr — If my records show I was in Texas at that time, would you disagree?
>
>Dameris — No.
>
>Carr — If others present at the New York meeting testify I was not there, would you disagree?
>
>Dameris — No.

Dameris actually had testified in a deposition May 11, 1971, that he had met me only twice, and both times were in the National Bankers Life offices in Dallas. "Would you say," I asked Dameris, "that your recollection at that time, being less than one year after your trip to New York was more reliable than it is today, almost four years later?" He replied, "Yes sir."

I also proved from my records that I was in Dallas July 8, 1970, and Osorio and others who had attended the meeting testified I was not in New York. I had escaped another trap.

Although behind-the-scenes maneuvering never let up, the trial had developed into a humdrum affair for the press. Ruth Eyre of The Dallas *Times Herald* wrote that it was "cranking along like a re-run of an old movie. . . . Testimony in the case now on trial seems to have raised less notice than a sneeze in a hurricane."

Four days after that story, however, Robert Watson pulled another of his stunts when he called a press conference to announce he would file suit March 10, 1974, against Republic

National Life Insurance Co. of Dallas. I thought it was a stunt because of the timing. It doesn't take a genius to realize what effect such a suit might have on jurors in a similar case. The timing, of course, could have been circumstantial had they been naive people, but they weren't naive people. The SEC used an unprecedented maneuver by calling a press conference to say they were going to file the suit. Also, the jury was not sequestered, and you have to presume they hear talk about these things: bad loans, misapplication of funds, manipulation of stock and so forth.

I asked for a mistrial, but the judge denied my request, saying he felt he had "adequately" impressed upon the jurors that my case must be decided on the evidence produced in the courtroom. I could only hope he was right.

Mahony was becoming increasingly frustrated in his failure to connect me with what he claimed were illegal activities. Once a government witness testified that he had sent a letter to the president of RIC International to try to close a business deal. Under my cross-examination, however, the witness admitted he had not sent me a copy of the letter. On re-direct, Mahony asked the witness, "Did you know Carr was vice president in charge of acquisitions for RIC?" The witness said he did not. Mahony, red-faced and angry, exclaimed, "I bet you would have sent him a copy if you had known he was." Taylor promptly instructed Mahony not to make a statement like that again before the jury. On the 15th day of testimony, Taylor, who was placid and, I thought, overly patient, flashed anger in rebuking Mahony publicly. "I want you to know I am not very happy about the posture the government has put on this case," Taylor said.

My associate, Travis Shelton, asked Taylor to put Mahony and Kiser on the stand to clarify what evidence their witnesses would present. Shelton said this preview would allow the judge to decide whether it was relevant. Mahony protested that this would be an "improper precedent." He said he would need approval from the U.S. attorney general in Washington before he could take the stand. Taylor denied Shelton's motion.

The government scored a psychological victory, however, after Colvin had told the jury that one of the government witnesses had lied with the full knowledge of the government.

Mahony immediately filed a written complaint with the Grievance Committee of the Dallas Bar seeking to disbar Colvin. I think it was ridiculous—they weren't going to get Emmett disbarred or reprimanded, because he had a reason to say what he did, and he had a right to say it in open court. But it really shook Emmett up.

Nevertheless, Colvin raised sufficient doubt about the witness's testimony that it probably had some effect on the jury. This, coupled with the admitted forgery of Osorio's signature on a letter that was important to the government's case, helped us immensely. In 1970 Robert Watson of the SEC had confronted Osorio with the letter, and Osorio said the signature did not look like his. Watson demanded that Osorio give him samples of his handwriting, and Osorio wrote his name three or four times on a piece of paper, which became part of his deposition. Now, more than three years later, the government was prosecuting this indictment based upon the same letter. Colvin secured a handwriting expert, James Lewis, a former U.S. Secret Service agent who had worked as a documents examiner since 1939. He testified he was of the opinion the signature was forged. The government's cross-examination of Lewis was meager, and on final argument, Stephens conceded that the signature was forged. Apparently the prosecutors had either not taken the time to check the signature or had gone ahead and used it with the knowledge it was forged.

On Friday, before I was to testify Monday, Mahony objected that I should not be allowed to testify in a narrative fashion as I had—I thought effectively—in the first criminal trial. We were all hovering around the judge's bench so the jury couldn't hear us, and Taylor, without listening to my argument, ruled that questions would have to be put to me by another lawyer. I had had no indication the judge would require this, and I was genuinely irritated. I was tired, emotionally drained, and to have this burden put on me over the weekend, where I had to keep my lawyer working, paying him and straining to get ready, was almost too much. I had to pay Shelton several hundred dollars extra in legal fees, but he handled the situation beautifully.

My watch read 11:08 a.m. when I walked to the stand on March 28, 1974, to tell my story. It was the 21st day of the trial.

My demeanor was one of complete confidence and belief in myself. Then, and during the cross-examination by Stephens, the jury seemed to be hanging on every word, but I didn't have a chance to study them because I had to defend myself against a tiger that was trying to chew me.

After my testimony, several character witnesses testified for me, and I shall always appreciate their presence. They were John Powell, a Dallas businessman with whom I worked while I was president of Universal Magnetics, Inc., a subsidiary of RIC; Grover Sellers, former appeals judge at Tyler and former Texas attorney general, who was retired; Albert Jones, the University of Texas law professor who had been first assistant attorney general; Robert Smith, district attorney of Travis County; Chris Hanger, assistant district attorney in Harris County; Travis Ward, Dallas businessman and civic leader; and Robert Storey, former president of the Texas and American bar associations.[1]

Our presentation ended at 2:40 p.m. April 1. My main misgiving was that the judge had refused to allow me to introduce testimony to support my claim that the indictment had been politically motivated.

Final arguments began April 5, and Mahony argued for one hour, but it seemed like a lifetime. He accused me of participating in a conspiracy to defraud and pillage banks, stockholders and the government, using imagery and gimmickry, lining my own pockets and stealing. He denounced me as a "common criminal" and demanded the jury find me guilty. The penalty could be as much as 14 years in jail and $35,000 in fines. The AP reported the "jurors sat in rapt attention ... while Mahony went through his emotionless summation," and, believe me, I was raptly watching those jurors' expressions to see if he was getting to them. If he was, I had an additional worry.

McCown had come to listen to Mahony's argument, but he hastened out before I made mine.

There had been heated discussions as we were trying to decide in what order defense counsel would speak to the jury. I wanted to be last because I had confidence I could do a good job, and I thought I was the best speaker of all of them.[2] Colvin said he would never agree to that because I might say something harmful to Osorio and Colvin wouldn't have a chance to patch it up. I was upset, but I couldn't let it go to where we were fighting among ourselves at the last minute, so I gave in.

As I do in every trial, I had outlined points on a sheet of paper that I wanted to cover, and I made notes on Mahony's argument that I wanted to refute. I've never been able to make a memorized speech, so on an occasion like this, I just talk from the heart. Once I get started, my enthusiasm feeds on itself, and I'm able to put in the right words and the right emphasis and to make gestures automatically. I never worry about it. I just live it.

This, in part, is what I told the jury:

> I must say that if there is anything worse than sitting on a jury for six weeks, it's being a defendant for six weeks. I want to say one other thing in explanation. I have been a pretty solemn fellow through this trial. I have not found much to laugh at. I have observed others in the courtroom being frivolous at times, but there is a difference. They are talking about names; when they call names, they are calling me names. It's my future, it's my life, it's my respect, my name, my reputation. To them it's hanging another scalp on the wall, a victory, a pat on the back for winning, just a job. To me it's everything. I never heard a man outside Mahony call me a criminal. I walked through the jungle of Texas politics for 17 years, not one scandal, not one scar. Suddenly in 1972 the Justice Department in Washington starts calling me a criminal. To them I reversed 52 years of life and suddenly I became a criminal in 1972. Before this is over, I hope I can show you the significance of that. The Justice Department is something besides the fountainhead of justice lately.

In every criminal trial I have ever been involved in, I approached the jury with a great burden on my shoulders: my client could be confined in the penitentiary; he would have to leave his family and friends; and he would lose his profession and everything dear, if he were found guilty. But when you're the fellow who might go to the penitentiary and lose your family, and you're arguing your own case, it doesn't take much to rev you up. Here I was within minutes of being permanently silenced, where I could say nothing else. At that point, I would have lost all control over everything, including my future. I would be putting my life in the hands of strangers.

The AP said, "Carr's fury seemed on the raw edge of control as he talked to the jury. Sneezes and coughs in the cavernous courtroom occasionally broke the silence like cannon fire." I felt like a caged animal. It was the end of the road. This was my last chance to tell the prosecutors off. To them this was a magic, magnificent marble game where I was the taw, and I didn't appreciate the odds. Like Monday morning quarterbacks, they were saying that decisions I had made were not only wrong but were fraudulent and criminal. I had stood weeks of that, three years of it; I had won one trial. I had one decision to go, but if I lost it, I might as well not have won the first one, because I would have to go to the penitentiary, I would be kicked out of my law profession, I would be parted from my family, I would have nothing left, no reputation, no future. I had to convince the jury, if it wasn't convinced already, that Waggoner Carr was an honest man.

> The Justice Department and SEC [I told the jury] kept me in public shame and ridicule for three years. It's not easy for a proud man to go through that. But there's one thing they will never do. They'll never break my fighting spirit. I'm fighting them now; I'll be fighting them tomorrow. I'll fight them as long as they're trying to get me, because I know they are wrong. What they have done to me, they can do to others, and when they use the power of government to do this, we have no more freedom. We have no liberty. We might as well be dead.

In retrospect, it seems anti-climactic, but I also told the jury that those were the last words I would get to say before they decided my fate. "Come back and say: Waggoner Carr is Not Guilty," I said.

"Watergate" was never mentioned by name.

The jury began its deliberations on Saturday, April 6. I remember the jurors asked a question of the judge pertaining to Osorio only, and it indicated to me that they had already made up their minds about me, but they recessed until Monday.

We spent Sunday at the Holiday Inn on the Central Expressway. Good friends of mine, Billy Mitchell and John McCann, ran that Holiday Inn and the one downtown.

On Monday, I resumed my wait, accompanied once again by Ernestine; my son, David; his wife, Diana; Mr. and Mrs. Fred Pryor of Dallas; Pryor's business associate, Brent Fawcett, and others. I paced the hallway, returned to the courtroom, sat down, got up, made conversation, always wondering—what is the problem? Why are they taking so long? Surely they don't think I'm guilty? Under such circumstances, only the man on trial knows the emotional stress that goes with waiting for that knock on the door that indicates the jury is ready to announce its verdict.

At 5:35 p.m. the word was passed that the jury was ready to report. The tension really hit the ceiling. Federal Judge Robert Hill was standing in for Taylor, who was out of the city at a judges' convention. As the jurors marched in, I watched their facial expressions, trying to get some kind of friendly feeling. They were obviously happy and relieved that the trial was over, but they didn't tip off their decision.

Hill, in a cool, solemn manner, asked each defendant to stand. Making every effort to appear calm, I rose. As the judge looked at the papers handed over from the jury foreman, I studied his face but he had no expression. It was deathly quiet in the courtroom. My head was heavy, and I was so tired. As he began reading—"Not guilty," "Not guilty," "Not guilty"—my tenseness diminished, and gradually I felt that everything was going to be all right. Hill read "Not guilty" to each charge, and my tiredness was gone.[3] I glimpsed the prosecutors as they lifted their briefcases and hurriedly left. The first emotion came from Travis Shelton, who let out a quiet sigh. Moments later, I shared tears of joy with my family and friends.

Reporters and photographers were waiting in the courthouse lobby, and now that I had finally proved beyond any doubt that I was innocent—and my accusers seemed to have vanished—I didn't mind the bright lights and questions and all. They were welcome. I said the verdict was "a great relief. I feel I've cleared my name. I will try to re-establish my law practice." A reporter asked me if I would try to seek public office again, and I said:

> A man my age has to think first of supporting his family. This has been hard on me financially. There are some people who always believe the bad and don't want to believe the good and so from those quarters, if I submit myself to political contest, I'm sure I'd have trouble. If a charge of wrongdoing is made against you when you're in politics, there is always a certain element of people who believe it; there's that element who will hear the charge and never hear the acquittal. The fact that you were indicted means guilty to a lot of people, and they will say you got out on some trick or a lawyer got you out. It's not right, but it's a fact of political life.

That night Ernestine and I went with some friends to celebrate. David and his wife, Diana, were with us and the Pryors and Mr. and Mrs. Tommy Butler and some of the corporate officers in Butler's firm. He's chief executive officer and chairman of the board of National Data Communications and was my campaign manager in my 1966 Senate race against Tower. It was a happy time, but it was not a hilarious time, rather a kind of controlled enjoyment. The tension was almost gone, but I was still very much involved in the trial in my mind and it was going to take me a while to adjust to the fact that it was all over. I didn't stay out too late; none of us did.[4] I was too exhausted.

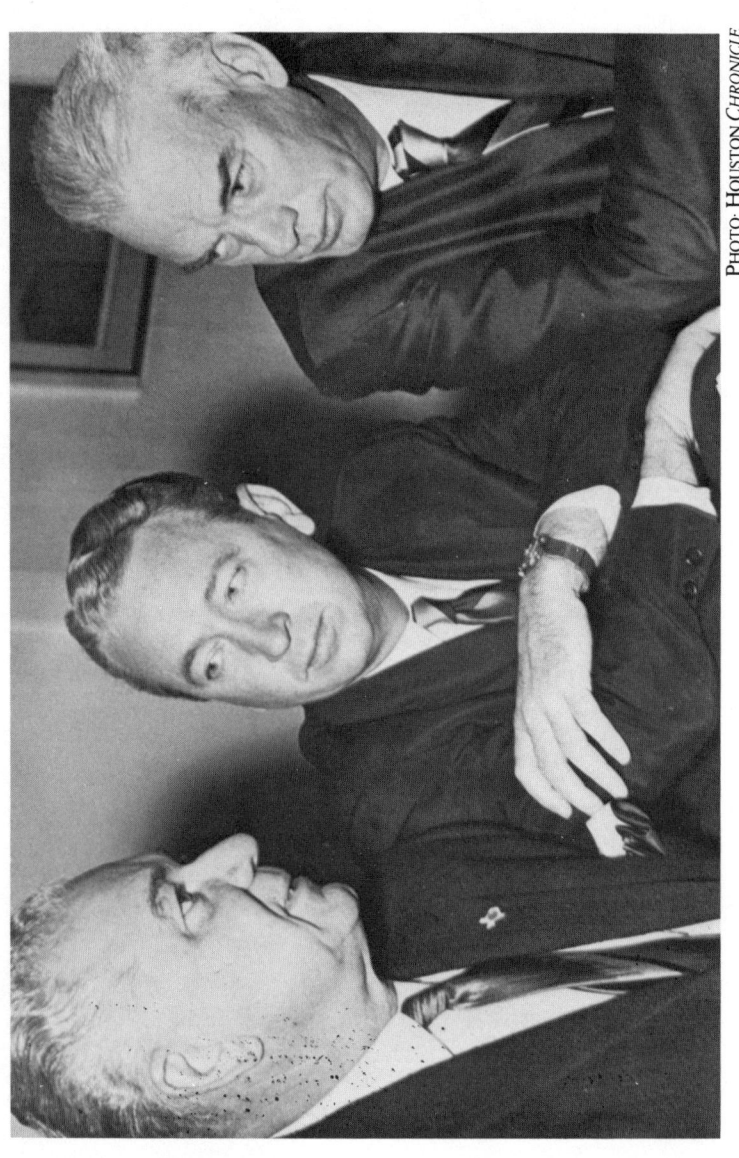

One of the many people who congratulated Waggoner Carr after his second acquittal was Leon Jaworski (left), special prosecutor of the Watergate investigation. This picture was taken in 1966, when Carr was attorney general. On the right is then-U. S. Representative Bob Casey of Houston.

Photo: Houston *Chronicle*

16

A Living Example

Two days later, the Lubbock *Avalanche-Journal* said my relief at being acquitted was "shared by his many Lubbock friends who have known him and believed in him all his life."

> The inclusion of Carr's name in broad brush allegations gave government investigators an explosive and dramatic way to 'break' the so-called Sharpstown scandal of 1971.... Now, three years later, it is perhaps significant to note that the Justice Department, despite a grant of immunity to the central figure in the whole case in exchange for the 'evidence' he could provide, has failed miserably to give enough evidence to the original insinuations to get a federal conviction against a single Texas officeholder.

I was particularly pleased that the Lubbock paper had supported me. I considered Lubbock my hometown even though we had not moved there until 1932, when I was 15, after my father's little country bank at Fairlie in Hunt County had gone broke in the middle of the Depression. We moved with the most meager possessions to Lubbock; we were very, very broke.

I moved from there officially in 1961 when I was elected attorney general, because the law requires the attorney general to live in Travis County.

I had always been popular in Lubbock, although I lost the county to Tower in the 1966 Senate race. I think I'm correct in saying that was not an anti-Carr vote but a vote against the Democratic administration.

While I was basking in satisfaction over the editorial, Bob Smith, who had the reputation of being a relentless prosecutor, told a reporter he wasn't surprised at my acquittal.

> It was inconceivable to me that he [Carr] could knowingly become involved in a criminal situation. My experience with him as an employee was that he was a person of the highest integrity—one of the highest I have ever met.[1]

No greater compliment could have been paid me.

When I asked Bob to be a character witness at my trial, I could only speculate that the jury would remember that he had prosecuted Gus Mutscher in the Sharpstown scandal, and yet here he was, defending me.[2] I could not remind the jury that he was the same man that had convicted Mutscher, just that he was the district attorney in Austin, where I lived. I thought I'd be extremely lucky if any jurors put the two together.

I met Bob at his house on a weekend, and I tried to make it clear that I did not want to put him in a position where he would be criticized for testifying to my good character; but I told him I needed him. I thought he might be subject to criticism from two sources: one, from those who would feel it was somewhat of a compromise of principle against the whole Sharpstown scene, and two, from longtime political enemies of mine who lived in Austin and who would find any excuse to bring pressure on him to let me go down the drain. He had no hesitation, however, about agreeing to testify. He told me it was because, as attorney general, I had not asked him as an assistant to compromise in the prosecution of slant oil well suits even though oilmen had supported me in my race. "I found out right then," Smith said, "that you were an honest man, because you never told us what to do and you accepted every recommendation we made."

The only person who declined to testify on my behalf was Mrs. Homer Garrison, the widow of the former director of the Department of Public Safety. I had often introduced Garrison at banquets as the "J. Edgar Hoover of Texas," and I was a great supporter of his. I asked Mrs. Garrison to go to Dallas because she was fully capable of knowing me, and she was a lady and I wanted a lady because there were lady jurors. She said she would be willing to send an affidavit and asked if that would help, and I said no. "Well," she said, "let me think about it," but I never heard from her again. It could be that the thought of going into court scared her.

Dallas *Times Herald* reporter Ruth Eyre wrote after the second trial of my "charisma . . . friendliness . . . and oratory."

A few oratorical achievements, at least, are a matter of record. My brother, Warlick, and I started debating together at Lubbock High School, and we had good success traveling all over the state. We got to regional competition in the University Interscholastic League contest before Amarillo beat us. We were the varsity team at Texas Tech and became the college debate champions of the southern United States. We supposedly had the best record of any debate team in Tech's history. As law students at the University of Texas, we didn't have the time to enter into much of the debate competition, but we were intramural debate champions and got a medal. That was the end of it.

Of the many congratulatory letters and telegrams I got after my acquittal, one came from Leon Jaworski, special prosecutor of the Watergate investigation, who wrote in longhand:

> Dear Waggoner: I have been in Texas for only a brief time—but long enough to receive the glad tidings of your acquittal. It proves two things: first, that you were innocent and next that you were a damn good lawyer. Jeannette and I rejoice with you and Ernestine and wish you the best of luck.
> Your friend, Leon.

We were close friends. For several years, a law associate of his, Wiley Caldwell, had been my principal campaign leader. He had been helpful in raising funds as well as being on my strategy council. This helped me stay close to Leon, and we really began to work together when he agreed to be one of my two special counsels in the Texas investigation of the Kennedy assassination. We made numerous trips to Washington together, attended social meetings, and I've been in his home.

Along with the congratulations, I got several invitations to speak, and I accepted them. I felt I had an obligation to tell my story. The first one was in Lubbock at a luncheon sponsored by the professional journalism fraternity, Sigma Delta Chi. The public was invited, and it was fully covered by television stations, radio and newspapers; we had a sellout crowd. It was a very emotional thing for me, because I was still somewhat fragile in my emotions and had not settled down from the trial. I was quite moved by the warm and friendly turnout.

There was also a warm crowd when I spoke to law students at the University of Houston. The dean was there, and again we had TV and newspaper coverage. One student suggested that I had disproved the maxim that a "lawyer who represents himself has a fool for a client." I told him to the contrary I would be the first to admit my client was a fool, but I added with a smile, "my client had a hell of a lawyer!"

The reason I felt I needed to keep these engagements was that I had a long road back to travel, and I didn't have much time to do it. For three years the overwhelming publicity had been hostile, I thought, and I learned in politics that unless you repeat, repeat, repeat, you don't get the ear of people like you think. This repeated attack against me for three years, I felt, had tarnished my name with people that one headline of acquittal would never reach.

Fortunately, the audiences were ready to accept my story. A tale of political prosecution was not far-fetched to them; it was not like trying to sell them a new bar of soap.

I remember so well when I was subpoenaed to go to grand jury meetings in Houston, and an FBI man would be in the witness room who would treat you like dirt, as if just because you had been subpoenaed, you were guilty. It permeated the room and made me want to wash my clothes when I got out of there. There are still some other individuals from that period that I'd just as soon not ever see again, but I am not the slightest bit interested in revenge. I developed a psychological approach during the trials that they could be and should be a very beneficial thing to me if I could meet the challenge and come through them. I've always felt that the best men were those who had come through adversity and won, that it had built conviction and self-confidence and made them more understanding of the problems of humanity.

I also felt that if my adversity had been caused by those who had abused the power the people had given them, then it had happened to me for some reason. Perhaps it was up to me to raise the flag of danger about government abuse of power against defenseless citizens. If I just went back to my law practice or went back and lived in a cave, I'd be betraying myself and, if I might say so, my country.

During those dark and troublesome three years, I often wondered, "Why me?" Gradually, I came to feel there must be a reason. All my adult life I had made laws and enforced them. Could it be that I was now being molded for a different purpose in life? At first, such thoughts were intriguing but hardly serious. Then, as I was buffeted by strong forces which I could neither understand nor explain, such philosophical thoughts became more believable. They helped me withstand the pain and misery. They gave me a kind of direction. My lonesomeness became more bearable. My belief that I would survive became firm. Hogwash? Perhaps to you. Not to me.

I had defeated my enemies. I felt a warm closeness to other Americans who know that they, too, have suffered abuse from their own government. I had the new confidence of a man who had accomplished something big and worthwhile. Also, I had lived the life of an "accused." I had been blamed, embarrassed, laughed at, schemed against, ridiculed, and spiritually crushed. I had been indicted and made to stand in a courtroom where a judge said if I were convicted, I could be caged for more years than I had life to live. I had heard the loud thumping of my heart when the jury foreman handed the verdict to the judge. Although the verdict was "Not guilty," I still remember how I shuddered as if I had brushed against the gates of hell on earth.

From this I emerged a different man—a man with more compassion and understanding. This test that I had passed sharpened my professional ability and my determination to use that ability to help others who I felt were being treated wrongfully by men armed with the massive power of government. I had learned how extremely fragile our personal freedoms and rights are when those in power want to take them away. Lastly, I gained a new regard for our jury system of justice. Not until I reached a jury "of my peers" was I rescued. It is the most perfect way imperfect man has found to judge the actions of other men.

Although I treaded water for three years, my time wasn't completely wasted. My trials and experiences gave me a platform from which I can tell you and others who may think it is preposterous that, under our form of government, an American citizen can lose his constitutionally guaranteed rights and privileges, that you are dead wrong.

If we don't keep a watchdog attitude toward our government and those who run it, such episodes, such abuse, will happen again. I want to make sure you know. I already know. I am a living example of it.

NOTES

CHAPTER ONE
The Hottest News Around

[1] Newspapers that had speculated favorably on my re-entering politics included the Houston *Chronicle,* The Dallas *Morning News,* Lubbock *Avalanche-Journal,* San Antonio *Express,* Longview *News-Journal,* Kilgore *News Herald,* Corpus Christi *Caller-Times,* The Houston *Post* and San Antonio *Light.*

[2] William P. Hobby Jr. won the race without Republican opposition after defeating Wayne Connally in a runoff in an eight-man Democratic primary.

[3] Sanders lost to Republican Senator John Tower in 1972 after winning the Democratic nomination over former Senator Ralph Yarborough in a runoff. Tower had defeated me in 1966.

[4] I felt at the time, as I still do, that Barefoot's real reason for declining to help me further was his plan to enter the approaching campaign for U.S. Senate against Senator John Tower. His decision was a wise one, for even as little as he participated in my defense, he must have regretted it. As the Democratic opponent to Tower in 1972, he faced a well-financed and relentless campaign, no small part of which was the radio commercial which said that Barefoot had represented a former Speaker of the House in the stock fraud scandal. This advertisement could make voters think he had represented Speaker Gus Mutscher who, by that time, had been convicted of bribery conspiracy. Technically, the commercial was correct in that some ten years before I had been Speaker of the House.

CHAPTER TWO
Lonesome Man

[1] Baum was the governor's hand-picked state party chairman. He resigned October 11, 1971.

CHAPTER FOUR
Good Bill

[1]Mutscher resigned as Speaker after he, Shannon and S. Rush McGinty, a Mutscher aide, were indicted on charges relating to conspiracy to accept bribes in the form of bank loan-stock profit deals in 1969 from Sharp in exchange for help in getting the banking bills approved. Mutscher, Shannon and McGinty were convicted by a jury in Abilene in 1972. Each was placed on probation for five years.

Nevertheless, Mutscher sought re-election to the House in 1974 but was defeated in a runoff primary by Latham Boone III, who himself was defeated in 1976 by Bill Keese. Boone blamed his defeat partly on Mutscher supporters who voted against Boone to get revenge.

[2]In "tagging" a bill or resolution, a senator requests a 48-hour notice of a public hearing on the measure. Since 48-hour notice is impossible in the last two days of a session, the delay can kill the measure.

CHAPTER FIVE
Some Kind of Deal

[1]While Shivers was governor, Osorio was on his staff, and he had always had great respect for his former boss. Osorio testified that although he was being asked to perjure himself, he wanted to think about the offer because he considered the threat of additional indictments as a threat on his life since he would be fighting the indictments for many years. Shivers correctly advised him not to commit perjury.

CHAPTER SEVEN
My Appeal Fails

[1]To show how the charges hurt Carr's law business, in 1975, after he had been cleared, he made $74,343.

[2]President Nixon's victory in Texas over Senator George McGovern was the greatest presidential triumph ever recorded in the state by the GOP, in counties captured, total vote, and ballot percentage. Nixon received 2,293,231 votes, or 65.25 percent, compared with 1,159,532, or 33.49 percent for McGovern. Nixon carried 246 counties and McGovern eight.

CHAPTER EIGHT
"The No. 1 Case in the Nation"

[1]I was indicted in July 1972, less than a week before the Legion convention was to be held in Houston, and I resigned from the race,

throwing it wide open. News of the indictment dominated the convention; everything was turmoil. There had been a small corps of Legionnaires, since Judge Hughes's decision, that wanted me to get out of the race, because they thought I was a crook and would give the Legion a bad name. But the leadership of the Legion had made it very clear that I had their confidence, and I would have been elected without any major problems had it not been for the indictment.

[2] I later got a print of the photo from Marshal Clint Peoples.

[3] Republicans in the House increased from ten to 17 and in the Senate from two to three.

CHAPTER NINE
"A Fool for a Client"

[1] The full firm name is Cantey, Hanger, Gooch, Munn & Collins.

CHAPTER TEN
There Always Was Tomorrow

[1] Taylor denied a motion to transfer the trial out of Dallas because of the pre-trial publicity.

[2] It was brought out in later testimony that McCown had told my former law associate, Tom Thomas, that if he could recall something that might incriminate me, the government would allow him to plead to one count; otherwise, he could be indicted on several counts. Thomas refused the offer and was named in a multi-count indictment.

[3] Ruff later became special Watergate prosecutor during President Ford's administration.

[4] "If I'd bought off Barnes, I'd have told them so," Osorio told the Associated Press, "but I didn't. They said they thought I was lying."

[5] I learned later that soon after the jury began its deliberations at 1:30 p.m., a preliminary vote was taken and it was nine for acquittal. Three of the jurors did not understand some of the testimony and asked questions of the other jurors. The next vote was unanimous—Not guilty! Before reporting to the court, however, the jury took a coffee break. It seemed that two women jurors had been told by their employers to come back to work if they were dismissed by 4 p.m. By waiting until 4:20 p.m., they got the rest of the day off.

CHAPTER TWELVE
Crack In The Door

[1] Tower was the ranking Republican member of the Senate Banking Committee, which had jurisdiction over all legislation affecting the SEC.

[2]Thomas was later indicted twice by federal grand juries that had worked with McCown and Kiser.

[3]The expense to the government to get witnesses to Dallas, Taylor said, should not be unreasonable considering how much it had spent in bringing indictments against me and the other defendants.

CHAPTER FIFTEEN
An Honest Man

[1]Storey's credentials also included chairman of the board of the Southwest Law Foundation at Southern Methodist University; special counsel on the Texas investigation of the assassination of President Kennedy; and a leader in the Nuremberg war trials following World War II.

[2]Carr and his brother, Warlick, were debate champions in high school, college and law school.

[3]I found out later the jury had quickly decided that I was innocent but had hung up 11-1 on issues that did not involve me.

[4]One of the most gratifying experiences, after my final trial, occurred when my son, David, tried to slip into class late the next morning. He had overslept, and he went in the back door to avoid walking in front of the professor and students. Apparently they had been waiting for him, and they all rose and applauded. It was a tribute, some told him later, for the way he had stuck by me.

CHAPTER SIXTEEN
A Living Example

[1]When I was attorney general, Bob Smith was an assistant and prosecuted the slant oil well cases.

[2]With time to think, I have decided that if I had been tried at the time Mutscher was, I probably would have been convicted, because the pressure of public opinion was still fever high. There had not been time for things to begin to settle where people were thinking sanely again. When I was tried, things had had two years to cool down, two years for Watergate to come along, and people had begun to make sense out of it.

INDEX

Abilene: 118n
Adams, Paul Jr.: 11, 13, 27, 29
Alexandria, Virginia: 72
Amarillo: 33, 54, 98, 113
American Bar Association: 11, 105
American Legion of Texas: 42, 45, 118n-119n
Anderson, Godfrey: 59
Arizona: 44
Arkansas: 26
Armstrong, Anne: 85, 98
Ashby, Lynn: 30
Associated Press: 2, 41, 46, 59, 101, 105, 107, 119n
Association of Old Crows, Dallas-Fort Worth Chapter: 79
Athens: 54
Atlanta, Georgia: 41
Austin: 1, 7, 18, 30, 37, 40-42, 46, 49, 56, 58, 64, 68, 79, 80, 96, 112
Austin *American-Statesman*: 18, 24, 41
Austin *Times*: 23

Baldwin, Bruce: 52
Barnes, Ben: 1, 6-8, 22-23, 30-31, 40, 47, 55, 66, 68-70, 72, 79-80, 85, 89, 93, 98, 119n
Baum, Elmer: 9, 20, 47, 55, 72, 117n
Baylor University: 61
Beaumont: 87
Bentsen, Lloyd: 90, 98
Birdwell, Jerry: 53, 72-73, 76, 79
Blue Cross: 62
Boltz, Gerald: 36-37, 39, 68-69, 80, 92-94
Boone, Latham III: 118n
Bowers, A. S. "Sid": 10

Braniff: 16
Bristol, Ted: 71
Brown, Richard (Dick): 18
Butler, Tommy: 109
Buzhardt, J. Fred: 98

Caldwell, Wiley: 113
Cantey, Hanger, Gooch, Munn and Collins: 49, 119n
Carr, David: 61-62, 108-109, 120n
Carr, Diana: 62, 108-109
Carr, Ernestine: 1, 16, 42, 47, 60-63, 108-109
Carr, Osorio, Palmer, Long and Coleman: 2
Carr, Warlick: 44-45, 49, 51, 53, 55, 97, 113, 120n
Casey, Bob: 110
Central Expressway: 55, 108
Christian, George: 98
City Bank & Trust of Dallas: 15, 20, 56
Clines, Robert: 80
Coleman, James: 40
Colson, Charles: 98
Colvin, Emmett: 53-54, 66, 72, 74, 79, 83-84, 93, 103-104, 106
Commerce Street: 97
Committee of 100: 10
Committee to Re-elect the President: 7, 45, 73, 80, 98
Connally, John: 7, 96
Connally, Wayne: 117n
Cook, Bradford: 64, 80, 98
Corpus Christi *Caller-Times*: 117n
Cotton Bowl Association: 58
Cox, Archibald: 98

121

Crump, David: 27
Curtin, Mary: 98-99

Dallas: 1, 4-5, 11-12, 14-15, 20, 26, 30, 32-34, 42-43, 45-46, 49, 52-53, 57-58, 61-62, 67-69, 78, 81-83, 92, 94, 97, 100, 102, 105, 112, 119n-120n
Dallas *Morning News*: 10, 21, 26, 35, 41, 55, 65, 67-68, 117
Dallas Public Library:97
Dallas *Times Herald*: 23, 41, 102, 113
Dameris, Thano: 101-102
Dean, John: 72-77, 79, 98
DeLay, John: 11, 13
Democratic National Committee: 98
Department of Public Safety: 34, 112
Depression: 111

Enemies List: 98
Erickman, Mr.: 90, 92
Erickson, Ralph: 30, 84
Erlichman, John: 98
Ervin, Sam: 86, 95, 98
Evans, Rowland: 75
Eyre, Ruth: 102, 113

Fairlie: 111
Farris, Anthony J. P.: 26, 29, 74, 80, 84-86, 89-91, 98
Fawcett, Brent: 108
Federal Bureau of Investigation: 25, 39, 65, 72, 80, 87, 114
Federal Deposit Insurance Corporation: 19-21, 68, 70-71, 80
Fifth Circuit Court of Appeals: 39
First Bank of Houston: 27
First National Bank, Dallas: 44
First National Bank of Lake Jackson: 27
Ford, Gerald: 119n
Fort Worth: 1, 4, 9, 11, 25-26, 39, 49, 68, 71, 80
Fort Worth *Star-Telegram*: 41-42
Fortune: 73

Franke, Alton: 80
Franks, Zarko: 64-65

Garrison, Mrs. Homer: 112
Geary, Joe: 27
Geary, Brice, Barron and Stahl: 26
Geddes, Tom: 42
George, Ronald: 56
Gibson, David: 85
Golz, Earl: 41-42, 68
Gonzalez, Henry B.: 29
Granger, Ned: 18, 23-24
Gray, Patrick: 65, 72-73, 76-77, 86-87, 98
Green, Bill: 58
Grievance Committee of the Dallas Bar: 104
Guy, Charles: 42

Haldeman, Robert: 98
Hanger, Chris: 58, 105
Harper, Fred: 68
Harris County: 105
Heatly, Bill: 20
Hill, Jerry: 90, 92
Hill, Robert: 108
Hobby, William P. Jr.: 117n
Holiday Inn: 34, 55, 108
Holladay, Truman: 29
Hoover, J. Edgar: 87, 112
Houston: 3, 5, 10-11, 16, 26, 28-31, 33, 39, 53, 64, 68-69, 75-76, 80, 91-93, 101, 110, 118n
Houston *Chronicle*: 4, 41, 64, 68, 117n
Houston *Post*: 4, 30, 35, 41, 117
Hughes, Sarah T.: 1, 5, 11, 13, 16-17, 25-27, 32, 34-36, 39-40, 119n
Hundley, William: 87-89
Hunt County: 111
Hunt, Howard: 98
Hunter, Ed: 41

Internal Revenue Service: 39, 80
International Life Building: 1

Jaworski, Leon: 11, 110, 113
Johnson, George: 41
Johnson, Lyndon: 47-48, 98
Jones, Albert P.: 58, 105
Jones, Bob: 37, 39
Junell, Frank: 10
Justice Department: 21, 25, 29-31, 34, 39, 41-42, 44-45, 51, 53, 72, 74-77, 79-81, 84-87, 92, 98-99, 106-107, 111

Keese, Bill: 118n
Kennedy, John: 11, 113, 120n
Kennedy, Robert: 87
Keumpel, George: 18, 23
Kilgore *News Herald*: 117n
King, John L.: 61
Kiser, Lawrence: 25, 44, 53, 71, 74, 98, 103, 120n
Kleindienst, Richard: 29-30, 44, 46, 65, 67, 74-75, 80, 82-87, 90, 98
Krogh, Egil: 98

Lake Jackson: 26
Lamon, Robert: 99, 101
Langston, Lonnie: 56
Lewis, James: 104
Liddy, Gordon: 98
Life: 73
Ling, Michael: 8
Longview *News Journal*: 117n
Louisiana: 26
Lubbock: 33, 44, 47, 49, 51, 56, 111, 114
Lubbock *Avalanche-Journal*: 42, 111, 117
Lubbock High School: 113

McCann, John: 108
McCowan, Frank: 30, 41-42, 44-45, 53-56, 58, 67, 71-72, 74, 80, 90, 97-98, 105, 119n-120n
McGinty, Rush: 118n

McGovern, George: 118n
McLane, Bonner: 41

Mafia: 45
Mahon, Eldon: 39-42
Mahony, Robert: 44, 53, 59, 67, 72-74, 98-99, 101, 103-106
Maroney, Jim Jr.: 41
Master Control, Inc.: 16
Merritt Schaefer & Brown: 46
Mitchell, Billy: 108
Mitchell, John: 7-8, 64-65, 67-68, 72-74, 77-79, 82-83, 87-89, 94, 98
Mitchell, Martha: 98
Mollenhoff, Clark: 25-26
Morehead, Richard (Dick): 10, 21
Morse, Bill: 5
Mulloy, Patrick: 46
Mutscher, Gus: 20, 58, 70, 89, 112, 117n-118n, 120n

Nashwood Corporation: 15-16
National Bankers Life Insurance Co.: 1, 8-9, 16-17, 45, 55, 58, 101-102
National Data Communications: 109
New Orleans: 39
New York: 88-89, 101-102
Nickles, Mrs. Pat: 60
Nixon, Richard: 4, 7, 11, 47, 65, 72, 74-76, 79-81, 85, 87-88, 93-94, 98, 118n
Northern Judicial District: 33
Novak, Robert: 75
Novotny, Joseph: 8, 53-54, 56, 80, 90
Nuremburg: 120n

Oak Forest Realty Co.: 16
O'Connell, John: 51
Odessa: 37
O'Donnell, Peter: 10
Office of the Special Prosecutor: 98
Ohio: 26, 30-31, 93
Ormand, Jarrell: 99

123

Osorio, John: 8, 16-17, 20-21, 23, 33, 45, 53-56, 58-60, 66-67, 70, 72-73, 80, 85, 93, 98, 102, 104, 106, 108, 118n-119n

Palmer, Eugene: 19-20, 71
Patman, Bill: 23
Peoples, Clint: 119n
Petersen, Henry: 44, 72, 74-75, 84-86, 98
Pickrell, Robert: 44-45
Pinson, Theo III: 30, 80, 84
Powell, John: 105
Proctor, Les: 37, 39, 97
Pryor, Mr. and Mrs. Fred: 108-109

Republic Bank Tower: 13
Republic National Life Insurance Company of Dallas: 102
Republican Policy Committee: 79
Reynolds-Penland: 46
RIC International Industries, Inc.: 8, 15-16, 56, 58-59, 61, 103, 105
Rice Hotel: 64
Richardson, Eliott: 98
Ruckelshaus, William: 98
Ruff, Charles: 30, 55, 72, 74, 79, 84-85, 119n

St. David's Hospital: 18
San Antonio: 16, 29
San Antonio *Express*: 117n
San Antonio *Light*: 117n
Sanders, Barefoot: 4-5, 11, 117n
Saxbe, William: 93
Scovell, Field: 58
Seaman, Richard: 41
Securities Act: 10, 15, 93
Securities & Exchange Commission: 1, 4-5, 7, 9-12, 14-17, 19-21, 23-27, 30-31, 33-37, 39-40, 44-45, 55, 61, 64, 68-69, 73, 76, 80-81, 87, 92-94, 98-99, 104, 107, 119n
Sellers, Grover: 105
Senate Banking Committee (U.S.): 119n
Sentinel (Airlines): 40
Serino, Robert: 30, 84
Shannon, Tommy: 20, 118n
Sharp, Frank: 8-9, 16-17, 19-21, 28-31, 33-35, 38, 40, 53-56, 69-72, 74-77, 79-81, 84-88, 90-93, 98, 118n
Sharpstown: 58, 67, 69, 74, 79-80, 83, 86, 89, 94, 111-112
Sharpstown State Bank: 8, 19, 21, 29, 53, 69, 93
Shelton, Travis: 49-51, 53-55, 88-89, 100, 103-104, 108
Shipley, H. A.: 54
Shivers, Allan: 16, 20, 30, 118n
Shumway, Devan: 80
Sigma Delta Chi: 114
Simpson, Mrs. T. R.: 37
Sims, James: 30, 69
Singleton, John: 29
Smith, Preston: 1, 10, 19-21, 40, 47, 55, 72, 89
Smith, Robert (Bob): 58, 105, 112, 120n
South Atlantic Corporation: 8, 15-16
Southern Methodist University: 11, 58, 120n
Southwest Law Foundation: 120n
Stakem, Richard Jr.: 80
Stans, Maurice: 98
State Banking Board: 19, 72
State Bar of Texas: 51
State Democratic Executive Committee: 47
Stephens, Richard: 98, 104-105
Stewart, Robert: 68, 80, 93
Storey, Charles: 11, 13-16, 26, 29, 36, 39-42, 44
Storey, Robert: 11, 58, 105, 120n
Story, Mrs. H. C.: 40
Strauss, Robert: 98
Stromberger, Ernest: 23
Strong, Jack: 23
Susman, Morton: 31, 70, 90

124

Tahoka: 51
Taylor, William Jr.: 46, 49, 53-56, 58, 60-61, 65, 67, 74-75, 79, 83, 86, 94, 101, 103-104, 108, 120n
Ten Most Wanted Men: 45
Texas Bankers Association: 21
Texas Democratic Party: 77
Texas Department of Public Safety: see Department of Public Safety
Texas House General Investigating Committee: 30
Texas House of Representatives: 4, 10, 21, 47, 117n-119n
Texas Observer: 30
Texas Press Association: 33
Texas Radio and TV Association: 41
Texas Senate: 10, 21, 47, 119n
Texas State Network: 4
Texas Technological University: 10, 47-48, 113
Thomas, Tom Max: 71-72, 77, 99, 119n
Thompson, Quinton: 68-69, 80
Timmins, Tim: 31, 42, 44-46, 49, 69-70
Tower, John: 2, 6-8, 11, 47, 65, 68, 77-79, 89-90, 98, 109, 111, 117n
Travis County: 18, 58, 105, 111
Travis, Robert: 46, 49
Tyler: 105

United Press International: 41-42
United States Department of Justice: see Justice Department
United States House of Representatives: 29
United States Secret Service: 104
United States Securities and Exchange Commission: see Securities and Exchange Commission
United States Senate: 2, 8, 78, 87, 90, 96, 109, 111
Universal Magnetics: 105
University Interscholastic League: 113
University of Houston: 58, 105, 114
University of Texas at Austin: 47, 58, 113

Victory Dinner: 1-2, 4, 68
Vietnam War: 2

Wall Street Journal: 73
Ward, Travis: 58, 105
Warner, Phil: 41
Washington, D.C.: 5, 11, 25-26, 29-30, 34, 42, 44-46, 51, 53, 55, 67-68, 74, 77, 79-81, 84, 86-87, 94, 97-99, 103, 106, 113
Watergate: 45, 64, 67, 74, 82-83, 87, 94, 97-98, 107, 110, 113, 119n-120n
Watson, Robert: 1, 15-17, 26, 44, 68-69, 74, 93-94, 102, 104
Watson, Steve: 9, 27-28, 68
West, Dick: 65
White House: 72-73, 77, 79-81, 85, 87, 98
Wichita Falls: 4, 49
Willeford, George: 10, 79, 85, 98
Wilson, Charles: 23
Wilson, Will: 8, 11, 65, 72-77, 85-89, 93, 98
Wood, Sam: 18
Woolf Brothers: 46
World War II: 120n
Wright, T. B.: 58

Yarborough, Ralph: 117n
Zimmermann, Julian: 7-8, 68, 89

125

13116
9 50